Staffordshire Library and Information Services
Please return or renew by the last date shown

If not required by other readers, this item may may be renewed in person, by post or telephone, online or by email. To renew, either the book or ticket are required

24 Hour Renewal Line
0845 33 00 740

Staffordshire
County Council

www.staffordshire.gov.uk

A FREE SPIRIT

Gives you the right to make choices

BETTY SHINE

HarperCollins*Publishers*

HarperCollins*Publishers*
77–85 Fulham Palace Road,
Hammersmith, London W6 8JB
www.**fire**and**water**.com

This paperback edition published 2002
4

Published by HarperCollins*Publishers* 2001

ISBN 0 00 653203 9

Typeset by Rowland Phototypesetting Ltd,
Bury St Edmunds, Suffolk

Printed and bound in Great Britain by
Clays Ltd, St Ives plc

If I have put into my book anything which can fill the young mind with better thoughts of death, or soften the grief of older hearts; If I have written one word which can afford pleasure or consolation to old or young in time of trial, I shall consider it as something achieved – something which I shall be glad to look back upon in afterlife.

The Old Curiosity Shop
Charles Dickens 1812–1870

CONTENTS

INTRODUCTION

The contents of all the chapters in this book have been chosen to enlighten and give hope to all who read them. At the very least, I hope they will encourage people in the very stressful society in which we now live to put aside a little time to think about the subjects that have been chosen.

I have always been able to communicate with creatures of all kinds. The natural environment is my real home, and my spirit returns there whenever I need to replenish my energies. If I am not in a place where I can see the sky and the horizon, I feel trapped.

As a child, I spent hours sitting at the top of an old cedar tree, gazing between the branches into space. Even then, I was aware of a presence that filled my body with a sense of peace. Intuitively, I felt that I should be 'out there', and not living on this planet. I know now that the links between myself and other dimensions were created and woven into the tapestry of my life, even before my birth.

That is why the spirit world made itself known to me at an early age. From just two years old, I could see and hear spirits: figures walking through my bedroom at night forced me to spend more time hiding under the sheets than I did lying between them.

My love of nature came from the hours I spent lying on the grass during the summer months, listening to the mysterious sounds I could hear emanating from the centre of the earth. I remember the bewilderment on my mother's face when I told her that I could hear the grass growing. When she questioned me further, I became excited, and told her that I could also hear the trees talking to each other. She just smiled, and patted me on the head. I am not sure why this particular incident should have had such an impact on me. Perhaps even at that young age I detected the disbelief I was later to accept as the norm whenever I spoke about these things to people who were ignorant of any other kind of world but the visible one – the world they could see and touch.

But communing with nature in all its forms – animal, vegetable and mineral – was a natural gift for me, and doubt in the reality of my own experiences, which can be a major factor in closing down a person's senses, was absent from my mind. The invisible world played an important part in my development, and the love and knowledge that were passed on to me were more important than academic qualifications. I used my intuition as a tool, and as a result I have been able to open doors that remain closed to others.

I have always accepted the natural gifts I was born with as my birthright. But who am I? Where did it all begin?

My paternal grandmother was a talented medium and dedicated Spiritualist. She was certainly different from other grandparents I knew. Tiny, with black curly hair, piercing eyes and little gold earrings that she wore constantly, she was a formidable figure. Nobody ever questioned her decisions – they wouldn't dare! I was always in awe of her, even though I was born under her roof and was part of her family.

Although she had given birth to thirteen children, only seven survived. But this was not unusual in the early 1900s. I think her suffering was eased by the fact that she was able to communicate with those she lost through her abilities as a medium.

I know nothing about my grandmother's background. But it was obvious to me that, somewhere down the line, she had come from gypsy stock. It was from this source that I inherited my talents: first the music, and then the mediumship and healing.

If my grandmother had not been such a strict disciplinarian, it might have been a typical Bohemian household. Her children were all talented artists, musicians and singers, and nearly every room in her large Victorian house contained a piano. This early introduction into the world of music, and talented musicians, has never lost its magic for me. Throughout my life, music has been my inspiration and has empowered me when I needed it most. It is a constant companion, which has helped me to reach for the moon when all other avenues have seemed to be closed. It has been my lifeline.

From the time of my birth I have never lived a normal life. I grew up listening to my grandmother talking to her dead children, to relatives and friends. There was no ridicule, just an acceptance in the family of the afterlife.

My paternal grandfather had a book which proved that his lineage went right back to the Hebrews. I was too young to understand the significance of this book, but I remember that he guarded it with his life. None of us could touch it, but I did catch a glimpse of it once. The cover was old, and the pages were brown around the edges, but it had an aura about it, and even at that young age I could feel the power that emanated from its pages.

It is only during the last twenty years of my life that I have given this book, and its significance, any thought. This is because of the amazing affinity there has always been between me and my Jewish friends. I have also had the privilege of healing Jews who were incarcerated in concentration camps, and through their stories I know that the world lost not only the innocents, but also great and good men and women of wisdom whose words were lost for ever – wise and gifted people the world could not afford to lose. The impact of this loss is still with us today, while an ever-increasing circle of violence still threatens to destroy the planet on which we live.

My mother's family were active members of the Church of England, and had very little to do with my Spiritualist paternal grandmother. Silent religious wars raged at the very core of our family life. This was very good training for a medium, because people are constantly trying to goad me into arguments of a religious nature. Many seem frustrated that I recommend that we all 'live and let live' rather than taking sides. If people are happy with the religion of their choice, that is all that matters. If for any reason their religion threatens to spoil their lives, they should leave it and seek a different path – one that gives them peace.

The local church played a major role in my mother's life. Although I hated it, it was a place where I was allowed to sing, and I looked upon that as some kind of compensation. Although I didn't know it at the time, it was to prepare me for my singing career later.

I know so little about my family because we lost contact with each other during the Second World War. I am obviously not a thoroughbred of noble stock, and I am truly grateful for this, because the road I was destined to walk has been long and hard. It also opened the doors of compassion and understanding and has enabled me to teach through the written word.

My ability to bypass the physical and link into the mind has also opened many other doors. My spiritual teachers taught me not to judge by appearance, because this life is only a coat that we wear for a short space of time, but to pay attention to the mind, which will continue to exist long after our physical presence is dead.

People who have communicated with me in order to give survival evidence have told me about their 'life after death' experiences and their surprise when they were asked by a 'Being of Light' what they had learned. Without exception, they have told me that this was the last question they'd expected to be asked, because they had thought that the afterlife was about the consequences of good and evil. As a result, they had all been afraid of the aftermath of things they had done that had had an undesirable effect upon those who were close to them. However, the question they were posed is proof indeed that life is about seeking knowledge if we wish to progress.

I hope that this account will have given you some insight into why I care so much for every living thing on this planet, and why we all have a part to play in resurrecting a healthy environment. This

book will take you further along the road of understanding, and I hope that that it will be a valuable
addition to your library of knowledge.

PART ONE

How to Communicate With All Life-Forms and Interact with the Environment

I live not in myself, but I become
Portion of that around me; and to me
High mountains are a feeling, but the hum
Of human cities torture.

Childe Harold
Lord Byron 1788–1824

CHAPTER 1

Animal Cruelty and My First Patient

I visited the circus for the first time when I was four years old – and I hated it. When the animals performed, I felt physically sick, and my heart filled with sadness at the sight of elephants, bears, lions and tigers performing tricks to entertain the public. I remember crying all the way home.

It was the same when I visited London Zoo. The sight of such majestic creatures pacing up and down on a concrete base, surrounded by iron bars, again tore at my heart. Their humiliation and pain became mine.

My family were mystified by my apparent distress. Although I was too young to understand or explain, I clearly remember that feeling of isolation and of being different. And so it has been all my life.

I spent many years wondering why I felt such intense pain on these occasions. And it was only from my study of the mind that I realised I had the ability to tune into the wavelength of every living thing.

11

To this day, humiliation and cruelty towards animals (and all other life forms) continues. Time and money are now being spent on trying to eliminate cruelty and extinction, and on improving living conditions in wildlife parks and modern zoos. However, in premises outside these establishments, there is still terrible suffering. In so-called civilised countries such as our own, cruelty towards animals who cannot defend themselves takes place on a minute-to-minute basis. Animal rescue centres are full of pathetic cases, and although television documentaries and series like *Animal Hospital* and *Pet Rescue* try to educate the public, there is still a long way to go.

Every single human being guilty of cruel behaviour demeans us all. I believe that the perpetrators of these horrors are mentally maladjusted people, social misfits whose numbers are unfortunately growing. It is tempting to presume that the abusers are all alcoholics and drug users, but I believe that the majority are people who want to take out their anguish on someone or something for a life that has gone wrong, and animals are an easy target. This will not stop until the laws are changed – it is still far too easy to maim and kill animals without having to face the consequences. Although these people may be banned from having an animal of their own for many years, it cannot compensate for the terrible death of even one such creature.

This could change tomorrow if everyone was vigilant and had the courage to speak out if at all worried about a possible case of cruelty or ignorance in the way a pet is being treated. I have heard about animals who have been left out during the winter, without any cover and with only soaking rags to lie on. Although Animal Rescue is notified, stupid laws often prevent them from helping, and the wretched animals continued to suffer.

Similarly, thousands of dogs are tied up in gardens. They howl all day, which is the only way they can ask for help – and they usually get a beating for it.

Mice, rats, gerbils, hamsters, rabbits and guinea pigs are bought to entertain children who quickly become bored with the effort of looking after them. As a result, these little creatures can be left imprisoned in small cages day after day. Unable to move freely, they show their deep psychological distress by going round and round in circles. These pets usually belong to families who show love for each other but who do not give a single thought to the torment that is going on within the mind and soul of the animal in their care. People should know better.

I have seen snakes who have never been out of the confines of their glass prisons, for that is all these containers are. They are often bought as a novelty – but novelties eventually lose their charm, and that is when the fate of the snakes is sealed. Never to be fed, cleaned or handled in a proper manner, or to

13

experience any positive vibrations, they surely must embrace death as a loving friend.

I wanted to be a vet but it was not to be. However, through the medium of healing I have been able to use my gifts in a more subtle way. Human beings are not superior, they are simply different. It is essential that we show some humility by meeting other species half-way. Only then will we be able to share their lives.

Animals do not understand our language, and for communication to improve we must learn to improve our telepathic abilities. Telepathy is simply an extension of intuition, that gut feeling which everyone has experienced.

Of course, it helps if you have been born with telepathic ability, but even psychics have to learn to adapt to things that are strange and difficult. Lessons have to be learnt, but once you have achieved your objective you will never lose the gift, it will be with you for ever. Individual effort helps make the world a better place for everyone.

If you are capable of compassion, then there is no reason why you should not be able to heal. Healing is a natural ability, born out of love for every living thing.

I was about eight years old when I practised healing for the first time. Walking to school one day, I saw a cat which was obviously in distress. I stopped and stroked it, and then held it in my arms. It just seemed the right thing to do. Then, in my head, I heard the cat speak to me, and I responded in the same way. I was too young to realise that I was having a telepathic conversation, and because of my religious upbringing I asked God to make the cat better. I stroked it for about ten minutes, and then hurried off to school.

The cat was still sitting in the same place at the end of the day, so I cuddled it again for a while before making my way home. As the cat had looked so thin and ill, the following morning I asked my mother to give me some scraps, but when I reached the spot where I had left it, it had disappeared, so I left the food on the ground. As I went home that afternoon it jumped out of a bush, climbed on to my shoulder and began to purr – a totally different disposition from the one I had left it in the previous day. I was delighted.

Some friends told me later that they had seen the cat being stoned by a gang of boys, but by the time they had returned with an adult it had been carried off in a sack. The youths must have dumped it on their way home.

Although still very young, I vowed then that I would try to make the world a better place for any animal that crossed my path. At that time I could not have foreseen just how involved I would become through the power of healing.

Most children are natural healers and have no problem communicating telepathically with their pets. But they become uneasy if adults don't understand, and they gradually lose the ability. If you watch a young child talking to a pet, you can sometimes see that the child is answering apparently inaudible questions. But if an adult is near, they will lose their spontaneity and reply in the spoken word. It is fascinating to study children in these circumstances, and we could learn a lot from them.

It is important that we do not lose the child within us, for it is only with the mind of a child that we can achieve the impossible. Why is this? It is because children simply do not know that they are not supposed to be able to achieve the impossible. Once doubt arrives, we can no longer work our magic, because the secret of life itself is steeped in magic.

And what can be more magical than the ability to connect with all the other species who share our planet? In the following chapters I will teach you how this can be done. Don't worry if you feel that you are not psychic and therefore will not succeed. All you have to do is to rid yourself of doubt – it is a negative companion, and if you allow it to enter into the equation you will fail. It is only 'knowing' that will unlock the doors of your mind and take you into realms of understanding that would otherwise be closed to you.

Remember, we are all born psychic, but if you

neglect any part of your wholeness, then you will lose that talent. Finding the keys once they have been lost can be difficult – but not impossible.

Share your soul with the animals and they will teach you everything they know.

I shall light a candle of understanding in thine heart, which shall not be put out.

The Bible
2 Esdras

CHAPTER 2

Communication With Our Pets

Before any kind of communication with wild animals can take place, it is first necessary to understand the domesticated pet. Most people believe they know what is going on in the mind of their pet, but unless they have a relationship where they are 'as one' with them, they are probably wrong.

All life forms have the ability to react emotionally to any given situation. Unfortunately, because animals do not speak our language, they can only respond to vibrations and sound. That is why pets in the home invariably show a lot of affection to their adopted families. Their ability to show this love may seem quite extreme at times, but that's because it's the only way they can communicate their feelings.

But it is the territory in between that is difficult to define, and an area which, if misunderstood, can lead to illness and possible death. The lives of our pets are in our hands. If they run away from a particularly bad situation they may end up being passed from place to place, which can often have disastrous consequences. Or they may not find a new home and be put to sleep. They have no hiding place.

If you can begin to have a 'gut' feeling whenever you are near your pet, you will be able to feel their emotions. But if you always insist on having things your own way, then you have lost the plot before you begin.

I have been in homes where owners have made it clear that their pet has to obey every command. This is sheer lunacy. They are trying to turn an animal into a robot. Of course there have to be rules, but they should never be so rigid that there can be no give and take. What about the times when the animals are feeling under the weather and cannot respond as usual?

In the country, many dogs are kept outside in all weathers, so when they are ill their suffering can be acute. I have seen the owners of these animals sitting in comfortable chairs by a warm fire on a bitter winter's night, with no thought at all for the poor wretched animals outside.

I know from experience that these people would never accept that they are being thoughtless and uncaring. Many of them come from families who have always treated their animals in this way. So it is only through education, through television and books, that children today are beginning to understand not only the laws of nature but also those of love, kindness and compassion towards the creatures who share this planet with us.

Before taking possession of any animal, it is essential to understand what will be involved in taking care of it in the proper manner. Because we have taken away its natural habitat and have tried to humanise it, we have become responsible for it. Although this may not be an ideal situation for human or beast, it is simply the way things are. But trust between our species can grow if more effort is put into the relationship by us.

Training an animal to fit into your environment must never entail any action that would harm the animal. Cruelty will only reduce the poor creature to a miserable, neurotic wreck. Worse still, those animals capable of attack will eventually retaliate, and then they might be labelled as difficult, impossible to train and not worth the effort, so they are put down.

It is not just animals who behave like this. Humans react in the same way when they are treated badly. But in their case, such behaviour will usually elicit support and understanding from friends and counsellors. Sometimes, if the animal attracts the attention of a caring organisation, then it will receive similar treatment, but a large percentage do not have this chance.

*　　*　　*

I received a letter from a woman who begged me to heal her Highland terrier. It had apparently taken an intense dislike to her lodger and become extremely aggressive whenever he was around. This was unfortunate, because he actually liked the dog and had tried to bond with it. She assured me that, apart from having bitten her ex-boyfriend – who hated dogs – it had always been very docile.

There is always a reason for aggressive behaviour in an otherwise docile animal, so I decided to set up a telepathic link whilst giving it healing. The result was rather surprising. The first picture I received was of a man's jacket and the feeling of fear the animal had whenever it came into contact with it. I received a strong impression that the jacket had belonged to the ex-boyfriend.

I contacted the owner, who not only confirmed my diagnosis, but told me that she had given the jacket to her lodger after it had been cleaned and that he always wore it when he took the dog for a walk. I was able to explain that the energy of the original owner would always remain in the fabric of the jacket, no matter how many times it was cleaned, and that her terrier associated the coat with its fear for the ex-boyfriend.

Wherever we live, whatever we touch, and whoever we meet throughout our lives, we always leave a part of ourselves behind – that part is the mind. Once you understand this, it becomes obvious that you must strengthen your own mind in order to counteract any negative vibes you may encounter. However, animals do not have this level of understanding, and so react instinctively.

With this diagnosis in mind, the owner destroyed the jacket, and all signs of aggression from the dog disappeared. A year later, I was delighted to learn that the dog and the lodger had become firm friends.

A lifetime of linking in with animals has taught me that there is always an underlying factor to unusual behaviour in our pets. It is not always possible to change the circumstances, but it *is* within our power to investigate every avenue, to try to uncover the underlying source that is causing the disturbance.

I remember one lady who had all the qualities necessary to ensure the happiness of a beloved animal. But she was taxed to the limit the time her dog reacted in a very aggressive manner when she moved house.

Her companion of five years was a collie cross. They went everywhere together, and the love they shared was there for all to see. She decided to move from her large rambling Victorian home to a small isolated cottage surrounded by three acres of fields. She thought it would be an ideal situation for her and her dog.

However, as soon as they had moved in, the animal's personality changed. It was no longer a loving pet but an aggressive and totally neurotic stranger. The local vet visited the dog, and also called in a dog psychiatrist, but to no avail. When all else had failed, the lady wrote to me, begging for my help.

I decided in this case that I would use remote viewing, which is the ability to visit places by using mind power. On my first 'visit', I was astonished to see a phantom figure standing behind the dog. I could feel the animal's distress as it tried to escape the attentions of this very negative spirit, who was haunting the cottage.

I made contact with the dog's owner and explained the situation, offering to exorcise her unwelcome guest. Understandably, the lady was shaken, but agreed to let me intervene.

I contacted the spirit and asked it to leave, to look for the light. But it took three sessions before the owner was able to inform me that her dog had returned to normal.

A year later, she happened to mention the incident to a near neighbour, who then told her that the late owner of the cottage had not only been extremely possessive of her home and belongings, but had always hated dogs. Everything points to the conclusion that it was she who was haunting her own cottage.

Because animals can see spirit manifestations, it is possible to determine where the spirit is standing by studying the animal's behaviour. If a dog feels that it is being threatened in any way, it will show its teeth and snarl, and even try to attack the apparently empty space occupied by the spirit. They can also feel the temperature dropping as the entity absorbs earth energies in its efforts to stay where it is.

My next story involved the whole of my family, including our own dog, Mickey.

My husband and I were looking for a larger house, as our children were growing up and we all needed more space. We looked around for several months before we found a house we liked. As it was obviously empty, we parked our car in the drive so that we could have a closer look. The large garden was overgrown, which was strange because it was in a very upmarket area and the surrounding houses looked immaculate.

We were about to leave when we noticed that the back door had been left ajar. Gingerly, we pushed the door open, and found ourselves standing in a huge kitchen. As we walked through into the hall, Mickey rushed past us, and then stopped in his tracks and began to whimper. This was unusual behaviour for him as he was normally a very confident dog. It was at this point that I felt a prickly sensation over the whole of my head – always a sign that something is wrong.

Determined to view every room, we investigated further, and found that all the walls in the house had oak panelling. This gave them a very sombre look, and for some reason it filled us all with a sense of foreboding. There also seemed to be a peculiar smell about the place like rotting vegetation.

Not wishing to leave until we'd looked upstairs, we tried to encourage Mickey to accompany us in case he strayed, but when we began to climb the stairs, the fur around his neck stood on end and he started to howl.

I asked the children to stay downstairs with him whilst my husband and I apprehensively made our way up the oak staircase. Off the long landing we found five bedrooms, two bathrooms and a nursery, and it was in this last room that we felt the atmosphere closing in on us. There was a strong feeling of evil, and on the floor and in the cupboards we found many discarded old toys. It was obvious that someone had left in a hurry. My gut feeling told me that something awful had happened in this room – it was time for us to leave. As we made our way back downstairs, I had the distinct impression that we were being followed, so we all made a hurried exit.

We later asked the estate agent who was handling the sale if he knew the history of the house, but he couldn't enlighten us. We also asked him if he had been aware that the back door had been left open. He said that he hadn't, and that he would see to it immediately. I felt he was hiding something from us in order to make a sale, but when it became obvious to him that we were not going to buy, he admitted that the place was haunted.

We were so fascinated by this house that we made a point of passing it whenever we were in the area. It remained empty for four years before it was finally demolished. Eventually another house was built on the same site.

I don't know whether the owners of the new house ever felt the negativity that had taken over the site. I would be extremely surprised if they had not, as it had seemed to have pervaded every inch of soil. As a medium, I have never underestimated such energies. That is why I avoid negative people and situations, for no good can ever come out of them.

Psychometry is the ability to divine and interpret the energies contained in an object. By holding something, the psychic can receive mental pictures of its history or about its owner. And, as incredible as it might seem, the pictures become clearer with age, which shows that the mind's essence is capable of growth as we get older. Using psychometry, it is also possible to receive pictures from the past history of a place – even a single grain of soil can contain the energies required.

If you want to check out whether a house is haunted or not, take a dog along with you, and if it growls or its hair stands up, then forget it. Some dogs may take a while before they react, but they will eventually, and it is at this point you will know it is time to leave.

Cats, on the other hand, root themselves to the spot when they are confronted by a spirit form, and their eyes form a slit and change colour. No matter how long it takes, they will sit like that until the entity disappears.

It is very important to create a bond with your pet so that you can easily interpret what it is trying to tell you. Many lives have been saved by animals behaving in such an odd manner that they have alerted their owners to a dangerous situation.

I remember one incident in particular. I was a guest at a garden party and the hostess had a small cairn terrier which never left her side and was normally well behaved. On this occasion, however, its behaviour had become so intrusive that she asked a friend to take it into the house. But the dog would not move. Then it began tugging at her dress. It was at this point she realised that something must be wrong, so she followed the dog as it led her towards the end of the garden. To her horror, she found that her two-year-old grandson had fallen into the ornamental pond. He was barely conscious when he was pulled out, and fortunately he recovered. There is no doubt that the terrier saved his life.

This kind of telepathic contact is typical when pets and their owners have a special rapport. The lady was able to read the signals she was receiving from her dog and acted upon them.

It is only by attuning ourselves to the natural world that we will be able to continue to co-exist with the animal kingdom. But there is a worldwide problem that threatens not only animals but humans as well, and that is ignorance. It lies at the root of all the needless cruelty we hear so much about and which demeans us all. When cruel and cowardly acts are perpetrated, whether against humans or animals, the law that governs the Universe will ensure that the perpetrators will pay a terrible price.

Although physical cruelty is horrendous, there are probably more cases of mental cruelty that go un-punished because they leave no physical scars. Owners with several pets might pick on one of them and use it as a scapegoat when things go wrong with their own lives. These people blame everyone but themselves for the bad things that happen to them, and a pet is a sitting target for their abominable behaviour. Even if these deeds take place behind closed doors, it is easy to recognise an animal who is being treated in this way; it looks cowed and unhappy, and is afraid to move for fear of reprisal. One can only imagine what it must be like for the one who is being victimised, especially when it sees the other pets in the household being shown affection and treated with care.

Children can also be extremely cruel to animals

and must always be supervised when a new pet is introduced to the household. If the pet shows any sign of reticence or distress when it is expected to play with the child, then something is happening that the animal doesn't like. Parents must always remain vigilant.

If it is the parents' choice to have a pet, then they must be aware that children can be extremely jealous of the newcomer, especially in the first few weeks when it may receive more attention than the child. It is a similar reaction to that caused by the arrival of a new baby. You simply cannot have too many discussions before choosing a pet, and every member of the household – including young children – should have their say. As young children can be very psychic, please give them your full attention, because their 'out of the mouths of babes' contribution could teach us all a lot. The whole family should collect as much information as possible on the kind of pet they want and determine whether or not they will be able to fulfil their duty towards the animal before they make their choice. Hundreds of pets die every year, not because they were not loved, but because the owners were ignorant of their basic needs.

I have seen goldfish in tiny bowls, swimming round and round in water that has no plants and therefore not enough oxygen. For these poor fish, death must be a blessed release. At fêtes, they are put into plastic bags and given out as prizes to small children who have no idea what to do with them. They nearly always perish. Just because it is cheap and is a great attraction to children, I have never been able to figure out what kind of adult treats a tiny life form in this manner.

Through my mediumship and healing, I have learned that everything we do to others will return to affect us no matter how long it takes or which dimension we may inhabit at the time. As human beings, we should all demand respect from others and be prepared to show that same respect to every living thing. Without that respect, telepathic contact cannot take place. Neither can it take place without the presence of love, compassion and patience.

I was contacted by a lady who owned a horse called Samson. She told me that bald spots were appearing all over his back, and that although he had received veterinary treatment over a period of five months, his condition was deteriorating. I told her I would try to help.

Although I do not need to meditate for the process to begin, I decided to do so on this occasion, as I felt there was a deep underlying psychological cause for this condition – to effect a cure, my mind would have to become 'as one' with the horse. The first impression I received was that the animal was extremely unhappy.

Gradually, I received pictures of all the staff at

31

the stables and one person came to the fore. As I watched the scenes being played out before me, I saw this person kicking Samson's legs, and as the pictures became clearer I could tell that it was a male member of staff and his name came through to me.

As the misery of the horse manifested, tears rolled down my cheeks. If horses could cry, then this one would have been weeping. In that moment of extreme love and compassion, I knew that I could help this animal.

The telepathic link was secured, and we 'talked'. Samson conveyed to me that this man was unbelievably cruel and had taken a dislike to him. I reassured him that I would do everything in my power to have him removed. I thought Samson also needed to be moved from that particular stable.

When I contacted the owner she was understandably mortified and promised to look into the matter. Within days she called me to say that the man in question had been dismissed. She thought that Samson would now be safe, and decided not to move him. I told her that I had made him a promise and that I hoped she would endeavour to keep it. I knew that the vibes around those particular stables would always affect him and that he would never fully recover if he was not moved to a more loving and caring environment.

I continued to give Samson healing for a month.

Each time I contacted him, I could still feel his despondency. At the end of the month there was suddenly a distinct improvement. He had been moved.

The owner admitted later that it had been difficult to find the right stables for Samson, but her patience had been rewarded. His coat not only returned to normal but now had a gloss that everyone admired.

Horses are sensitive and extremely telepathic – they are at their most beautiful when they are wild. When they are broken, their free spirit is crushed, unless a sensitive trainer can combine the exercises with extreme compassion and patience. Unfortunately, people like this are rare.

Experience of humans has taught every species to be afraid. That is why wild animals attack us. But there are isolated places in the world where there has been no human contact at all, and the animals there are completely at ease with the humans who are endeavouring to make contact with them.

With a little thought, less selfishness, and less greed, everyone can make a difference to this extraordinary and beautiful planet on which we depend for our survival.

In Nature's infinite book of secrecy
A little I can read.

Antony and Cleopatra
William Shakespeare 1564–1616

CHAPTER 3

Technology, Nature and Telepathy

In today's technological world we are beginning to lose touch with nature. At one time, the natural world and the supernatural were so closely linked that it was difficult to distinguish which part of the psyche was engaged in everyday life. Now people walk the forests, mountains and valleys armed with mobile phones. They lose the awareness of the audible silence that pervades the atmosphere and are unable to feel the vibrations of the living Earth and everything that is dependent on it.

We are in danger of becoming technological robots. Long ago, people were able to generate their own energy fields that interacted with the subtle forces of nature, creating zones where spirits abounded and magical moments were an everyday occurrence. When these things are absent, the world becomes a very dreary place indeed – pure black and white, with nothing in between.

Interest in science fiction is immense, not least

because such works offer readers a fantasy world where they can escape from the rigours of the real world. The danger comes when someone gives their whole life over to fantasy, neglecting their own unique creative imagination. The authors of science fiction and fantasy books and films are trying to use their imagination to stimulate the thoughts of others, not to imprison them in a single fake universe.

At some point we all need inspiration and, providing it does not become a habit, then that is the time when you can indulge in other people's fantasies.

Those of us who recognise the supernatural know that it can empower the imagination to such an extent that individuals begin to believe they can reach places where they would otherwise not have dared to go. The interaction we build up with other worlds at this stage is real, and therefore we don't need to lose ourselves in an imaginative process that has not been of our own making.

Imagination opens the doors of the mind so that we may see things as they really are and not as they *seem* to be. That is why I want to introduce you to the art of telepathy. And what better way could there be to begin than with animals?

I am often asked why the majority of people cannot communicate with animals. One answer is that they simply cannot be bothered to devote enough time and energy to it. The gift of communication with any species has to be learnt. Humans are encouraged from the cradle to learn how to interact with their own kind, but the same is not always true when it comes to interacting with the living world around us. There is one major difference between the two. Whilst we expect other species to respond to *our* language, the vast majority of people are not taught to meet the other species halfway. This is sad, because it can be done by using the telepathic ability of the mind. Although it takes time and patience, the end results are worth every minute spent learning this art. Not only will you be able to communicate with any creature, but you will also gain a better understanding of your own kind. Over the centuries, we have gradually lost our abilities in this area – through doubt and through the belief that man is superior to every living thing. We know now that this simply isn't true.

You only have to study ants to realise that their system of communication is impressive. They don't waste time or energy in achieving synergy with the natural world. I have been able to send telepathic messages to ants and have seen how these messages have been received and acted upon. They have an amazing ability to pick up on negative and positive vibrations.

You will see from the following story that, no matter how small or microscopic Earth's creatures might be, you can communicate with them in a way they will understand.

I received a letter from a couple who told me that ants had infested the plaster on the walls of their bedroom. They had tried everything possible to treat the problem, but without success. They did not want to use poisons because of the effect it might have on their small children. They begged me to help.

I asked them to find somewhere in their garden where the ants would be safe and where they would not cause any problems to them or the surrounding area. After much thought, they decided that an uncultivated area at the end of the garden would be the best place for them to go. With this in mind I could begin the process of moving the ants out of their old haunt and into a more suitable environment.

This is a common problem, and one that I had successfully dealt with many times, but I never take things for granted. The lines of communication I use are always the same, and I am never tempted to try to bypass these paths. Unless the message is powerful, the results will be negative – the message simply will not be accepted.

I focused on the address of the property then, using remote viewing, I entered the house and projected my mind into the bedroom where the ants were lodging. Using the power of my mind, I got an x-ray view of the activity behind the plaster. It was unbelievable – a black, pulsating mass of energy. I knew that if I doubted my ability to move this mass I would not be able to solve the problem, because doubt always counteracts our potential. I also know that if you allow yourself to be inspired by a challenge, then magical feats can be achieved and I love a challenge.

I began the process of driving out the ants from the plaster by building up a picture of one in my mind. Then I magnified the image. When I felt that the picture of the ant was secure and would not disappear, I spoke as I would if I were conversing with a friend. I knew there must be no anger in my communication, for this would have a negative effect upon them. I warned the ants that if they did not vacate the space behind the plaster, they would have no peace, but if they followed my instructions, I would guide them to a more secure site.

When I felt that the message had been received, I called the family and asked them to get in touch with me as soon as they saw the ants moving to their new home. Naturally they were sceptical, as they had never been involved in anything like this before.

The following day I received a call from them, informing me that the ants had gone. They had begun by moving across the room and out through the open windows. The family followed them down the garden until they reached the chosen site, and watched as they all disappeared underground. Apparently, it took four hours for them all to leave, but at the end of the day, not a single ant remained. Needless to say, the family was delighted with the results.

I know that this story must sound crazy to the uninitiated, but those who live an outdoor life and have an empathy with nature know that it can be done. I have received thousands of letters from people who would like to practise the art of telepathy but who are distressed by their inability to form an image in their mind's eye. They begin to feel that any kind of visualisation or telepathy exercises are beyond them, but this is not the case.

There is something I call 'knowing', and this is just as powerful as creating images. You *know* what you would like to see, and you *know* what you want to do. Once you have this confidence, the next step is to speak with your mind. It is as simple as reciting a poem in your head.

Each morning sees some task begin,
Each evening sees it close;
Something attempted, something done,
Has earned a night's repose.

The Village Blacksmith
Henry Wadsworth Longfellow
1807–1882

CHAPTER 4

The World About Us

It is impossible to communicate with animals unless you can 'feel' their world, an environment of sensation, vibration, scent, acute hearing and telepathic communication. It is virtually impossible for a human being to achieve all of these things at the animal's level, but with patience you can attain some of them in varying degrees. It really depends on how much time you are willing to devote to the project.

I have always been highly sensitive to different energy levels, all at the same time. The pull of one level tugging against another, and then the sensation of going into a slipstream, has been with me since birth. As a small child I was always aware of weather patterns and could forecast a storm three days before it arrived. But the first indication always came from the trees. I could feel them becoming more supple, as though they were shedding a certain rigidity. I knew that within hours they would begin to sway, even on a still day, as though in a light breeze, and at this point I would know a storm was imminent. When it arrived, the trees had become so supple that the branches would bend to a degree that under normal circumstances would have broken them in half.

I know now that the electrical disturbance in the atmosphere before a storm affects many people, but it is that extra *something* that makes one aware of the changes in all living things and able to understand the messages that are being transmitted through the ether.

Trees also know when they are to be felled. They absorb the content of the woodcutter's thoughts like a sponge, and they react accordingly. It is not only trees that respond in this way, but nature as a whole. Invisible, inaudible things are happening all the time between species, which enable them to interact with their surroundings.

One would think that you could get nothing from a stone, but stone circles – which were used for supernatural purposes in a past age – are particularly powerful and have been shown to have unique frequencies that cannot be found elsewhere. Whenever I visit the sites of ancient stone circles and place my hands on the stones, it is as if time is rolled back and I enter another age, and I can then perceive a life which was vastly different to the way we live now. If I repeat the process later with the same stones, I might 'timeslip' to an entirely different period. In the world of the supernatural there are no rules – it cannot be disciplined, and that is why I find it so fascinating.

On one occasion, whilst I was decoding the messages from a particular stone in the centre of a circle, I realised I could neither hear nor feel the frequencies that are so apparent outside of the circle. I made a study of this particular phenomenon, and had the same experience every time. This makes me believe that the stones themselves create a barrier, warding off harmful rays, and that is why I think I have found the centre of these circles to be so perfect for meditation.

Mobile phones disrupt normal frequencies to such an extent that their effects can be picked up not only by psychics but by people who have no aptitude for the supernatural at all.

I was walking along a cliff top one day with a friend who considered himself to be the most non-psychic person you could ever meet. He suddenly stopped in his tracks, telling me that he could feel something hitting the back of his neck. Minutes before this happened I had also felt a certain bombardment throughout my body. Looking back, we could see two people, both using mobile phones. We decided to stay where we were until they passed. Once they had disappeared into the distance, everything returned to normal. Since then, we have conducted similar experiments with friends, and the same thing happens every time.

My friend no longer believes he is totally non-psychic, but is a little shattered to find that he reacts so badly to something he cannot see. The most unbelievable things in this world are those that we cannot see, sense or touch – that is the magic which can, in an instant, turn your life around when you experience it for the first time. I pointed out to him that these energies affect every living thing, especially birds, who have to find their way through the tangles we have created in the Earth's magnetic circuit.

Animals, birds and insects are particularly sensitive to negative or black energies, and avoid areas where massacres have taken place – not massacres just of their own kind, but of humans too. Where terrible crimes have been committed, like the horrors that were carried out in concentration camps, the surrounding area is completely smothered by negativity of such a high density that it forms an indelible map which can never be erased. When in the future the whole world begins to use the psyche for survival, evolved humans will be able to read this map and wonder what kind of uncivilisation lived on this planet in earlier times.

The natural world inspires not only artists but those of us who want to interact and learn how to communicate with it. Like the human mind, the life force that surges throughout the whole of the natural world is independent of matter.

Through the systematic poisoning and destruction of the land, it has become increasingly difficult to maintain a healthy environment. Trees, plants, hedgerows and all living matter are affected. It is vital that each and every one of us should take into account the terrible damage that greed has done to our environment and reverse this trend where we can before more major disasters occur.

For centuries, Britain has had hedgerows, marking boundaries in a way that made our landscape look like a giant patchwork quilt. Small mammals, birds and insects found sanctuary in the tangled undergrowth, along with wild flowers that sheltered from the wind. Frogs, toads and other amphibians also sought shelter in the ditches that ran beside the hedgerows.

Yet over the past fifty years, the heart has been ripped out of the countryside. Now little over sixty per cent of these havens are left. Without the hedges, which act as natural windbreaks, winds have forged a path through crops and copse, causing considerable damage to the environment. Little thought was given to the consequences until it was too late.

Although farmers are now replacing some of the hedgerows, the land can never return to what it was before. The birds and other creatures which fed on and sought shelter within hedges have gone. Those which survived are few, and many have become endangered species.

The liberal use of poisons on the land has also affected humans, as the sickness in the soil reflects the sickness in ourselves. Over forty years ago, many people – myself included – did all we could to stop the use of DDT. At that time we were considered odd (at the very least) but we were right. Unfortunately, the greed had already set in, and more and more pesticides were approved and used.

It was clear that this insanity would gain ground, so I looked for a way to protect my family from harm and became a vitamin and mineral therapist. It was obvious to me, through study, that life-saving antioxidants were essential to healthy body maintenance.

At that time, whenever I introduced this subject into a conversation, people looked at me as though I was speaking a foreign language. Worse, they didn't care. Now antioxidants are being hailed as the new science and are being used to treat a host of major and minor complaints. If they had been introduced forty years ago, many lives would have been saved.

'You are what you eat' is a slogan that has been used many times to encourage people to cut out unnecessary (and possibly harmful) foods. But it applies equally to so-called healthy food such as fruit and vegetables when it has been grown on contaminated land. It is extremely difficult to find land that is clean, and in some cases it will take a hundred years or more for contaminated land to recover.

If they have a choice, animals, birds and bees will frequent areas that are undisturbed, because their natural instincts tell them that these places have not been contaminated.

Some farmers, who were considered too old fashioned when they kept to the old ways of farming, are now reaping the rewards. People are now prepared to pay a higher price for food that is truly organic, so that their children will have a better chance of health and survival. It is better to eat a not-so-perfect apple, grown organically, than the designer apple which may be suspect.

Wherever you are, even if it is in the heart of a city or at the top of a tower block, you can still close your eyes and allow your mind to visit beautiful places. Free your mind and you will open your life.

At one time I lived in the very heart of the country. Surrounded by trees, woods and valleys, it was easy to enjoy the beauty of all the seasons. But on one particularly gloomy day, I felt as though I needed something beautiful to brighten up my life, so I sat down and dreamed about the colourful birds that I had seen whilst meditating. I suppose my daydreaming lasted about fifteen minutes.

An hour later, I decided to pick some herbs for my dinner that night. I opened the door that led into the back garden and saw, sitting on a wall immediately in front of me, two of the most beautiful peacocks I have ever seen. Our eyes met, and we stood transfixed for about five minutes. Then I quietly moved into the main part of the garden. They didn't move an inch – and they never took their eyes off me the whole time. I stayed with the peacocks for two hours. Then, when I went back into the house, they flew away.

I lived in that house for four years, but I never saw them again. Then again, I never dreamed about birds from the spirit world again. Magical moments come in small doses, and I didn't want to push my luck.

To enable you to understand what it feels like to be at one with nature I would like you to take a virtual walk with me. First of all we are going to walk through some woodland.

Because it is spring, there is a feeling of expectancy in the air, and if you are intuitive you will be able to perceive this and absorb the energies. The crackling of the leaves underfoot will open up your senses to the past, and in doing so will automatically propel you into the future. For example, the very sound of the old leaves will remind you that in the previous year they had been fresh and green. Now dry and crunchy, they will decompose, adding nutrients to the earth which will then sustain the new life that is about to burst from the buds. If you close your eyes now, not only will you be able to visualise this, but you should also be able to hear it happening before the event. It may take time before you can experience this, but the more aware you become of your surroundings, and of the creatures that lurk in the undergrowth, the more it will become second nature to you to hear sounds and vibrations that have eluded you in the past.

The next step is to hold out your hands as you approach a tree. Take note at what point your hands begin to tingle. This way you can judge the health of the tree by the size of its aura. The size of the aura will also depend on the type of tree you are dealing with. As you get closer to the base of the tree the strength of the aura will increase, and if you lean against the trunk, you will feel the full impact. In summer, when there is a canopy of leaves, the aura will naturally become more intense, because every leaf has an aura of its own.

If you would like to experiment with self-healing, then you can do no better than to sit under an ancient oak tree. Noted for their longevity – a life-span of three hundred years in some cases – they also have magnificent auras. Their auras are so powerful that under favourable circumstances they can elicit a mental 'timeslip' which can allow you to decode the memory blueprint contained in the tree and propel your mind into a bygone age.

Once you are able to feel the aura of trees, you will be able to detect when they are diseased, even if there are no outward signs. Walking around the perimeter of the aura, slowly closing in on the tree, it is possible to make an accurate diagnosis and pinpoint the diseased areas. I have often used this method of diagnosis, and in many cases it has prevented the need to cut down the whole tree. It is also possible to use this process for the whole of nature, because every living thing has an aura.

Don't forget the birds that frequent these same trees. Each species has its own call, its own language, and yet they all have a sixth sense that enables them to understand and react to the whole. We have to make this sense our own before we can even begin to understand them.

When I was living in the middle of the woods, my garden was frequented on a daily basis by three types of woodpecker. The lesser-spotted woodpecker is tiny and secretive, so you are less likely to see it than the greater-spotted and green varieties. It was a joy to watch them as they took food from the bird table. In fact they were quite tame. This might have been because I used the garden for healing and meditation, which always casts a calm spell over the immediate vicinity.

Back to our walk. Whilst you are standing in the

middle of the woodland, close your eyes and visualise the bird you would most like to see sitting in the trees above you. Then imagine it in the palm of your hand. If your particular favourite has coloured feathers, gently move the feathers and separate the colours. This action will enable you to feel the heart-beat and warmth of its body. When you have inter-acted with the bird for several minutes, open your hands and let it fly away. From that moment on, the sense of belonging to the world of birds will be with you for ever. You might also want to repeat the process to bring back the magic of those moments.

Feathers themselves are fascinating. When you hold one in your hands, you will automatically stroke it. I know people who cope with stress by stroking their cheeks with feathers. They have strong associations – without them a bird could not defy gravity and fly above the Earth. They are symbols of a free spirit.

Try this exercise. Find one or two feathers – the size is immaterial. Stand out in the open, preferably on a hill, and hold the feathers in the air. Close your eyes, and when you feel a strong current of air, let them go, knowing that all of your problems are leaving with them.

Sometimes, rather than floating away, the feathers will turn around and drop at your feet. When this happens, it is a sign that you have to become stronger and more determined in your efforts to bring calm into your life.

Repeat the process until the feathers disappear. You will have taken the first step to inner peace.

Feather magic has been practised since the beginning of time. If you find a feather, make a study of the bird and its habits. You may find that the feather is trying to tell you something. For example, if you find the feather of a dove and place it on a table in the centre of a room, it will bring you peace. If you are lucky enough to find a feather belonging to a bird of prey, it might tell you that you need to be free of encumbrances, to soar above the earth, to find the stillness you seek.

The easiest way to achieve this is to meditate. Allow your mind to soar, to travel through invisible curtains which will show you that gravity cannot keep you locked in.

There are many pocket books on birds that you can buy, and reading through them can help you enhance the image whilst you're practising this exercise.

Here is a self-healing exercise. Sit under an oak tree, and feel the energy currents running through your body as you absorb the tree's aura. Then, holding a feather in your hands, take a deep breath and then breathe out through the feather, knowing as you do so that you are ridding your mind and body of toxins. This feather must never be used by others.

You can use feathers for physical healing too. You should keep a particular feather for healing, and store it in a box when it is not in use. When you need it, place the feather over the part of the body giving you a problem and blow through it.

To the uninitiated, feather magic might seem a bit far-fetched, but you'll never know whether it will work for you until you try.

I have spent many hours looking at the sparrow hawks that hover over the South Downs. Circular in flight, they climb into the sky then plunge to earth to claim their prey. For a long time I tried to imagine what it would be like to come face to face with this bird.

Walking into my conservatory one day, I saw a sparrow hawk sitting on a windowsill as if transfixed, and it looked at me with its huge yellow eyes. I stood quite still – in shock I think – because it was the last thing I'd expected to find inside my house. It was difficult to see how it had got in, as the gap in the door leading to the garden was so small. I believe now that it must have followed one of the many finches that sometimes found themselves in the same position whilst helping themselves to the bird seed that I stored inside the conservatory.

The bird was as beautiful as I had imagined, and I was loath to let it go, but because I had no idea how long it had been there – and thought that hunger must have caused it to get into this predicament – I knew I had to release it as soon as possible. Walking slowly to the door, I gently pushed it open and walked into the garden. Standing at a distance, I watched as the bird turned its head towards the doorway, then freed itself in a flash and disappeared behind a hedgerow, no doubt looking for its next victim.

Deciduous woodland has layers of vegetation which provide many different kinds of habitat needed to house the numerous species that dwell there. Scuttling in the undergrowth are shrews and wood mice, whilst badgers tunnel into the earth to create their sett, usually amidst elder trees which provide them with warmth, security and a safe haven within their intertwined roots.

A more common sight are the squirrels which perform their acrobatics in tree canopies. Their favourite venues are oak, sweet chestnut and sycamore in which to make their dreys, an untidy mass of twigs and dead leaves which are easy to spot in the winter. At night, the treetops are frequented by bats, which can be seen quite clearly at dusk.

On the edge of the woodland you will find hedgehogs, rabbits, hares, stoats, weasels and polecats. Hares love the open fields but are now increasingly taking to the woods in an attempt to preserve their own numbers.

If you live near woodland that slopes down to a river, you are likely to hear the nightingale singing day and night during the summer months. They migrate to Africa during the winter.

When your psyche opens up, enabling your mind to become a free spirit, you will be entering a magical world that will change your life. Becoming adept at visualisation will certainly make it easier for you to make contact with the wilder aspects of nature.

Whilst walking my dogs one day, I suddenly realised that it would be dark before I returned home. As there were no lights in the area, I made my way home carefully in the dusk, but as night drew in I stumbled across a rough field and fell over. As I got to my feet I threw my arms in the air and laughingly shouted, 'Let there be light!' Within minutes, I came across the longest line of glow-worms I had ever seen. I watched them for several minutes before resuming my journey. The light may have been minimal, but I thanked God anyway – at least He tried!

I walked this hill in the dark for many years but never saw the glow-worms again. When I was young, they could be seen everywhere, but now they are a rare sight, yet one more beautiful thing we have destroyed with insecticides.

The real challenge comes when you use your powers to try to out-fox a fox. This animal is naturally cunning and uses its coat – which has many variations of colour – as a camouflage. I have often caught a glimpse of one slinking through the undergrowth, and in the autumn they blend in perfectly with the changing leaves.

To mentally connect with foxes, you have to think like them, and occasionally I have been able to do this. One fox in particular used to frequent my garden and snatch the bird-cakes from a post near the house, even though I'd left food for it outside the gate. I tried to make contact telepathically, but to no avail. Eventually, I conjured up a picture in my head of an enormous hound dog with a fox in its mouth and sent the picture to the animal. Though it still collected food from outside the gate, it never entered the garden again.

With success comes the release of self-doubt, a negative attitude that prevents us from achieving the seemingly impossible. Many people have told me that although they would like to commune with nature, they simply don't have the time to sit and stare. But they are content to sit in front of their televisions and computers, and most of the time they are not achieving anything – certainly nothing that is going to last a lifetime.

Every individual must take on the mantle of responsibility for the health of our planet and for all the life it supports, otherwise the damage will spiral out of control. Time and time again I have been told that there is nothing that ordinary people can do to stop the decay. My reply is that there are billions of ordinary people who could turn the tide in any country if they were so inclined. The reason it doesn't happen is because there are too few people of courage prepared to save us from the disasters that threaten our environment, whilst the rest do very little or nothing at all.

Ecologists know what is going to happen. Others bury their heads in the sand, too lazy or too greedy to stop the rot that is threatening the whole world. People in previous generations who could have done something have ignored the issues until they felt their contribution would be 'too little, too late'. If we all do a little now, it need not be too late to save ourselves and our children from environmental destruction.

Man has been endowed with reason, with the power to create, so that he can add to what he's been given. But up to now he hasn't been a creator, only a destroyer. Forests keep disappearing, rivers dry up, wild life's become extinct, the climate's ruined and the land grows poorer and uglier every day.

Uncle Vanya
Anton Chekhov 1860–1904

CHAPTER 5

The Energy of the Natural World

The fact that we do not give enough time and effort to understand the natural world has always filled me with great sadness. We know it cannot survive if we continue to ignore the issues that are leading to the destruction of the world's ecosystems. It is becoming more and more difficult to reverse past mistakes, such as the continuing use of poisonous substances on the land.

Every particle of soil contains elements that are capable of transmitting messages from the physical to the spiritual realms. All living things interact with these subtle changes in the ether, and they are also sensitive to the electromagnetic fields around the Earth, and use them as a means of communication. It is these fields that are being distorted by the man-made wavelengths such as those used by mobile phones which enable humans to send and receive messages around the world in seconds.

Through my telepathic contact with wild animals,

61

I can sense a bewilderment among them that didn't exist thirty years ago. Back then a simple thought and image enabled me to send a clear message and receive a telepathic response. Now those images have to be clearer and more positive in order to counteract the years of ecological abuse.

It is possible for some species – including our own – to adapt, but it takes time. While we develop more and more advanced methods of communication, the distortion of natural energies in the environment increases.

Every living organism has evolved its own unique energy field, and it requires time and patience for us to even begin to understand this complexity. Unfortunately, time and patience are things that humans have in short supply.

The arrogance with which we treat this planet is there for all to see. The Earth is not a solid object but a palpable moving mass. When oil, gas and other fossil fuels are extracted and burned, the order of that mass changes, and this imbalance can cause terrible disasters around the world. Fortunately, animals react to the vibrations that precede natural disasters. For example, sometimes they leave the area two or three days before an earthquake. People living on fault lines watch their animals closely, and when the animals leave, they do too. Many lives have been saved in this way.

*　　*　　*

A friend of mine, who used to live in the region of a fault line in America, watched her dog so closely that they became totally telepathic. One day, whilst she was out shopping with a friend, she had a panic attack. It had never happened before, but it was so bad that she decided to return home. When she got there she found that her dog, who was usually very docile, was wailing and throwing itself at the walls of its enclosure. She let the dog out, but it tugged at her coat, trying to drag her away from the house. She realised then that something serious was about to happen and that her panic attack had been caused by a telepathic message from her dog. She dashed back inside the house, threw a few things into a suitcase, warned her neighbour, then drove away. It was only when she arrived at her sister's home fifty miles away that she relaxed.

Although she sat glued to the television for any news of a disaster, nothing was reported, and after three days she decided to return home. Whilst she was packing her case, her brother-in-law rushed in to tell her that there had been an earthquake in her home town and that several houses had been demolished.

My friend managed to get through to the local police, and was told that although her house was still standing, it had been badly damaged by falling debris. When she arrived home and saw the size and volume of the debris, she realised that she could have been killed. Her dog had almost certainly saved her life.

I believe that scientists should work with ecologists before they proceed with schemes that could further disrupt natural wavelengths. They may collect accolades for their inventions along the way, but if these same inventions create negative environmental results, even the scientists will not be able to escape the consequences.

Man cannot walk alone. For too long, arrogance and greed have killed and maimed those who are not rich enough to fight back. Honours should only be given to men and women who have tried to make this world a better place for everyone. Unfortunately, ordinary people and animals alike are being manipulated by minds which are not spiritually inclined, and in the end this can only lead to disaster – for both victims and perpetrators.

For example, the underground testing of the H-bomb has led to terrible problems for communities who depend on the products of the sea for their survival. In some areas coral reefs, which in the past have created safe havens for both humans and marine life, have been shattered and destroyed, and the whole ecological structure of these areas has been altered.

If this is happening in coastal areas near H-bomb testing, what is happening beneath the Earth's crust?

No matter how sophisticated our technology may be, it will never be able to stop the destruction of our planet whilst it is being abused in this way. Even though we cannot see what is going on in the centre of the Earth, that does not mean that it is safe. Earthquakes are becoming more frequent, even in areas that have never experienced them before, and if you follow the route they are taking around the world, it is obvious that geological problems exist that we can no longer afford to ignore.

The terrible tragedies being played out above ground are small compared to those we cannot see. They will surface in time, but by then it will be too late to turn back. We are seeing hurricanes and tidal waves, tornadoes and floods, and eruptions from volcanoes that have been dormant for generations. The list goes on and on. Some would argue that this is nothing new, that these conditions have existed since the beginning of time. But this kind of thinking is only evading the issue. The pattern *has* changed. Now there are too many catastrophes happening too often, and studies of these patterns suggest an urgency about the situation that we have never seen before.

Through my work I have seen the most appalling tragedies when it comes to 'pay-back time'. We all have to live with this thought, because Universal Law is unbending and unchanging, and it is a great teacher. In fact, it has been the only constant thing throughout my life. It has taught me that there is no hiding place. The justice given out by the laws of the land are a pale substitute for those we will eventually receive from spiritual sources.

Meanwhile, animals are suffering. Whales are washed up on beaches, miles from their usual habitat. When they are shepherded out to sea by the incredibly hard-working and compassionate teams of people who always turn out on these occasions, the whales will invariably swim back to a certain death on shore. Their natural radar – which has kept them out of trouble in the past – has been affected by unnatural vibrations above and beneath the sea.

Similarly, migrating birds are losing their way. Several species arrive at destinations that are foreign to them, and then have to contend with climates that cannot protect them.

Hundreds of these stories are brought to us on our televisions and in our newspapers every day. But what are we doing about it? Each and every one of us has to take an active part and participate in the discussions and decisions which at the moment are left to small minority groups. Otherwise the collapse of the Earth's structure will have a 'knock-on' effect on a scale we have yet to experience.

Take the time to study what is happening in your own country, and around the world. Whatever you do, don't put your head in the sand and pretend that it won't affect you, because it will.

*   *   *

Humanity has survived for well over 4,600 million years, in spite of the fact that it has experienced awesome changes – changes that have destroyed whole civilisations.

Long ago, people knew little of the world outside their own community, but within their own boundaries they instinctively knew that if they contaminated their surroundings they would die. In the forest, for examples, tribes would use a particular area for a time and then move on so that the region could regenerate.

Today, because of over-population, we all have to live amidst the rubbish heaps that are increasing in number and size every day. There is no place on earth that has not been affected, and yet it seems that governments around the world are still not prepared to spend enough money on environmental issues. The balance that sustains life on this planet is far more fragile than most people realise.

Acid rain is corrosive. It not only damages buildings but also kills trees, freshwater fish and vegetation. Two of the main sources of acid rain are the sulphur dioxide that emanates from coal-burning power stations and the nitrogen oxides from car exhausts. But how many people think about these issues? Most simply want to get from A to B as quickly as possible, no matter what the consequences may be.

Every nation needs to address these problems before it is too late. Damage to the ozone layer has already affected millions. People can no longer sun-bathe in safety because of the fear of contracting skin cancer, but little has been written about the way it has affected the rest of our lives. There used to be a time when summer vacations by the sea were relaxing and health-giving. This has changed dramatically. Now we are advised to protect ourselves by covering up, and to study the pollution charts to find out whether a particular part of the coast is safe for bathing. In fact, there are no *safe* bathing areas now, simply those that haven't quite reached the level of pollution considered to be dangerous to our health.

I was asked to heal the skin of someone who had been burned by chemicals whilst swimming in the sea. When his family investigated, they found that a factory was spilling chemicals into a river that led into that part of the coast.

I also saw a little girl who lost her sight because of polluted sea water, and it took several months of treatment before she regained full vision. She was lucky. Wind surfers too have suffered skin complaints after being in contact with sea water, even though they wear protective clothing. The list is endless.

Casualties are not only human, either. Thousands of fish are deformed and are chemically neutered, and so cannot breed, because of the hormones that are finding their way into the sea.

The latest news, in the year 2000, is that the

biggest hole in the ozone layer over the northern hemisphere will appear this spring. This means that Britain and Europe will be even more exposed to the harmful ultraviolet rays which cause ageing and skin cancer. Farming under these circumstances will be extremely difficult, as some crops will fail without the protection of the ozone layer.

From research commissioned by Friends of the Earth, it has been found that the air quality in Britain deteriorated in 1999 to its worst level for a decade. Poor air quality is estimated to cause 24,000 premature deaths in Britain each year. Traffic fumes have been associated with diseases ranging from leukaemia and other cancers, to bronchitis and heart disease.

Our lives will never be the same, and although we have to accept this now, it should never have happened. Fifty years ago, scientists were aware of the dangers we could face if industries went ahead with certain money-saving projects, but they decided to turn a blind eye. Instead, dangerous decisions have been made by people who have wormed their way into the inner sanctums of politics, simply to feed their own greed.

I find it laughable the way in which environmental issues are addressed in Parliament. If politicians make any useful contribution at all, it almost always carries a rider, which is that it will be dealt with in due course – anything from five to ten years hence or more. In that time we could all be dead! In this day and age, when technology is fast-moving and computers are out of date after only a few months, surely the people who govern should get a move on and not sit on the issues that can endanger lives?

Environmental issues should be at the forefront of regular Parliamentary debates, but instead they are put on the back burner. Many politicians are family men and women, and it is their children who will suffer. You would think that this alone would spur them on to defy opposition to any other dangerous issues that will affect the environment in which we live. But it seems that few are interested.

History repeats itself again and again, and we are told that governments have learned from the past. I fear they have not. You only have to consider the quotation at the beginning of this chapter, and note that *Uncle Vanya* was published over 100 years ago, to realise how ordinary men and women continue to suffer through the cunning and idiocy of the few.

We must try to reverse this state of affairs. In the first instance we can write to our local MPs – there are far more ordinary citizens than there are politicians, so we *can* make ourselves heard. And it takes so little time to protest in this way.

As far as environmental issues are concerned, it is my belief that everyone who wants to live in a safe and healthy environment should adopt the slogan 'Never put off until tomorrow what can be done today'.

70

The learn'd is happy nature to explore,
The fool is happy that he knows no more.

An Essay on Man
Alexander Pope 1688–1744

Getting Closer to Nature

The great thinkers of this world, past and present, are those who refuse to accept the obvious and who have absolute faith in their ability to look beyond the thought. This knowledge has given them the key to the invisible but inspirational place where thoughts are fine-tuned, enabling them to bring order to a disorganised world.

It may sound easy, but it isn't; to go down this road you have to be courageous enough to stick to your guns once you have made a final statement. There are millions of ordinary thinkers who have made a difference, so you do not necessarily have to have a great mind to bring about change. But you have to have the courage not to give in when you're targeted by negative thinkers who only consider themselves and their immediate problems.

It is important to read these words again and again before you continue. Not only are they the most important words you will ever read, but having read

...e visible and invisible lessons within ... will be inspired to think about everything ... you read and hear about in your day-to-day existence.

Lying to the country has always been a major political disease, and it continues to be so. Before television and this technological world that we now inhabit, the majority of people lived their lives in total ignorance. Nowadays there is no excuse for turning a blind eye to what we know is going on, and if you are a thinker, you will find that the obvious is constantly being used as a blind to hide the more subtle truth.

This is why I have dedicated the first part of this book to animals and the environment. Each and every one of us should be vigilant, for what is happening in these areas now will affect us all.

I have received far more sustenance from the invisible world than I have done from the material world. The secret is 'knowing' when you are in contact with something that you cannot see or hear. I call this the audible silence. You will soon be aware of the presence of invisible forces when you begin to receive inaudible inspirational messages which will impinge on the mind in your waking hours. Having once experienced this contact, you will never forget it.

Every medium and healer of any integrity has to be courageous when giving messages and when putting their faith in the spirit entities who become involved in the healing process. Early examples were shamans – natural mediums and healers who visited villages in the most outlandish places to pass on messages from the dead and to heal. They were revered and given a god-like status by those they served. Ridiculed by supposedly higher-minded individuals for imbibing large quantities of alcohol and herbal-based drugs in order to induce out-of-body experiences, they possessed talents that were nevertheless formidable.

There are those who have tried modern mind-altering drugs to achieve the same results, but it cannot work for them. The whole experience is not only spiritually orientated but earthed. Like all spiritual gifts, genuine shamanistic talents would have been there since birth. Though shamanism is becoming increasingly popular in this modern age, it does seem to attract dubious characters, so always get a recommendation before you choose a practitioner.

Many years ago, a colleague told me about the sangomas, who are traditional African healers. They are chosen from birth and spend a lifetime learning about the hundreds of medicinal potions that can be extracted from local herbs. They believe that everyone should be responsible for their own health, a belief I have advocated for many years. Through their spirituality, the sangomas are able to alter their state of consciousness to give messages from the dead and to read the future. Although they use bones, horns and the skin of animals, these trappings are merely a focus which links them to the natural world. Western traditions use other means: tarot cards, palmistry and runes are just three examples.

In our society, I would always recommend meditation as the only safe route if you want to experience the life-enhancing vibrations you get by raising your level of consciousness. Although it takes time to reach a stage of enlightenment (an advanced level of consciousness), it is well worth making the effort needed to reach this level. You will know you have achieved enlightenment when you begin to get clear, concise results which can be confirmed by some other means. At this point you will become your own gate keeper – you will automatically know who to let into your life and who to dismiss. The control will always be with you.

Some people need a focus for meditation, and like the shamans did long ago you can make your own. It could be in the form of animals or birds. The shamans used bone, horn, skin and parts of dead animals to bring them close to the soul of their chosen animal. The most popular totem was that of the Masked Sorcerer – half man, half beast. (You may prefer to use a pictorial image of your totem!) When the imagination is used in this way, there are no boundaries – the mind becomes a free spirit, and can move with ease from one world to another.

In our so-called civilised society, many would

think it rare for us to use animal totems, but this is not so. Photographs and television programmes have drawn us all into the world of animals, many of which we will never see in the flesh, but their images remain in our consciousness long after we have seen them. A photograph can be an extremely powerful totem, and although we cannot feel the skin of the living animal, I know through psychometry that the mind and soul of that animal – though invisible to the naked eye – is encapsulated in the image.

I receive photographs every day from people asking me to heal their pets. In most cases their vet has been unable to diagnose the cause of the complaint. I send them all healing, and wait for a favourable outcome.

One day I opened a letter that contained a photograph of a very sick-looking spaniel called Ricky. His owner had decided that if I could not help, the dog would have to be put to sleep. As I held the picture in my hands, I looked into his beautiful brown eyes and was immediately taken over by his mind-spirit. Through this medium, I was told that the dog had become ill when a pet rabbit he had befriended had died of natural causes. Ricky was heartbroken.

I called the owner and asked if the message I'd received was correct. They confirmed that Ricky and their pet rabbit had been inseparable and, after much thought, they were able to pinpoint the date when the dog had become ill – exactly two days after the rabbit had died. I told them that I had been able to tell Ricky that the rabbit was well and that they would meet again. Within a week the dog had recovered and was eating normally.

Those of you who have never communicated with animals may think this a tall story. However, those who are closer to nature will immediately recognise the interaction, not only between man and all other creatures but from one animal to another. I know from the thousands of letters I receive of the heartbreak suffered through the loss of a pet. I have no doubt that a warm-blooded animal feels the same gut-wrenching emotions.

If you want to have a closer and more spiritual relationship with the natural world, you will have to know how to initiate it. Ask yourself, which animal frightens you most? Think very carefully before you make a decision, because you will have to live with this animal for many months. When you finally make your decision, look for a photograph where you can clearly see every detail of the creature. There are many books and magazines that contain hundreds of photographs of animals, so this should not be difficult. A poster or a large picture from a calendar would also suffice.

The next step is to choose a wall in your home where you will be able to see the animal at all times.

Put up the picture, and whenever you have a spare moment, make a detailed study of it. Look into its eyes, talk to it, use it as a focus for therapy sessions. This will bring you closer, not only to the spirit of that particular animal, but to nature as a whole.

Variations in the colour of the animal's coat can help you to become intimate with the living essence of the creature. As you mentally part the fur to examine the variations, you will also feel the contour of its body and the warmth that emanates from it. Stroke the body with your mind, and 'feel' the warmth and heartbeat as you do so. Examine every part of the animal, from its shoulders down to its legs and paws. With the power of your mind, lift a leg so that you may look at the pad on its foot. The secret of becoming a soulmate with any living thing is to use your imagination, to move it around in your mind. When you do this you will create the feel and vision of a living, healthy and happy animal. Lightly draw your hands over the picture. Stand close to it, and look into the creature's soul. Use this as a meditation. After a few minutes, close your eyes and ask yourself what kind of emotions this act has aroused in you. Did you find that it had triggered an empathy you had never felt before? Could you see yourself cloaked in the spirit of a life which had appeared to be so different from your own? Did you have an overwhelming feeling that all life forms are the same when stripped of their physical appearance?

If you did not feel any of these things, then you have a long way to go before you can even begin to make contact with the different species that live on this planet. But take heart – it is only the beginning. You have done well to have taken the trouble to find a picture and study it. For each person who cares enough to begin the process, there are thousands who don't care.

However, when you have reached a point where you do feel at ease with your new friend, tell it that you will protect it and care for it as long as you live. With this vow will come a lifelong commitment and the knowledge that all life has a right to be here.

When you have accomplished the art of moving closer to something you had previously feared, seek out the real thing. If you have chosen an exotic creature, then you may have to pay a visit to a zoo or similar establishment. The closer you get to the real thing, the more you will learn about yourself. And having conquered one fear, you will know that you can do it again – not only with animals, but also with individuals of your own species. Fear undermines the personality, and you don't need this negative influence in your life.

Many years ago, I was staying at a monastery in Segovia, Spain, when I happened to see a young girl sitting on some stone steps, crying. I sat down beside her and asked if I could help. She shook her head and, with her hands cupped over her face, continued to weep. I put my arms around her, and as she relaxed she told me that she had lost her snake bracelet. I suggested that she could always buy another, but this only seemed to make matters worse. When I asked her what had been so special about that particular bracelet, she told me that it had special powers, and that whilst she was wearing it she had no fear of the snakes and scorpions on her father's land. I took her by the hand and retraced her steps, and within a few minutes we found the bracelet hanging on a branch of a lemon tree.

It was obvious to me that the girl had used the bracelet as a focus, to bridge the gap between the human element and the forms of life that she feared. This child had unwittingly stumbled upon an ancient ritual that turns an ordinary object into a living energy, which then creates a protective barrier around the owner. She had unknowingly created her own living charm. If we had not found the bracelet, she would have lost confidence and a certain amount of freedom until she had energised a similar object.

A close friend once told me that she was terrified of snakes. She hated the thought of anything slimy next to her skin. I assured her that she was mistaken, that the skin of a snake is dry and silky, but it didn't help at all. Even the thought of having a picture of a snake hanging on the wall disgusted her. I thought of the totems and how the shamans had made effigies of creatures from their skins, so I asked an acquaintance who happened to keep snakes if he would save me a shed snakeskin. Several months later he presented me with one, and I was able to arrange a meeting with my friend for her first therapy session. When she arrived at my home, I asked her to look at the snakeskin. At first she stood on the opposite side of the room, but with a little encouragement, she was able to get closer to the table so that she could see the skin. She was amazed to see how fragile and beautiful it was. Eventually she held it in her hands. I explained that part of the soul of the snake was in its skin. In tune with this spirit, she admitted to feeling guilty at having been so fearful of what was, after all, a living entity. Just because it was not human did not mean that it was any less valuable.

Much later, when I visited her home, I saw a brass snake on her windowsill. She told me that she had bought it when she finally realised that her fears had disappeared, after looking at a grass snake crossing the lawn in her garden. I knew then that something had touched her deep within her soul.

Having conquered fear, you will find the next step in your progression more to your liking. Choose a photograph of a beloved pet or a favourite animal and make eye contact with it. Then talk to it using words or silent thought – either way you will make contact. Take as long as you need to bring about the interaction between your mind and the mind of your chosen animal. Then close your eyes and listen. Although you may not hear words, you will 'feel' something – and that something will be different for everyone, because mind-to-mind contact is unique to the individual, regardless of whether it is between human and animal, human and human, or animal and animal. I have listened to thousands of stories of first impressions gained when practising telepathy for the first time – the following is a guide to what you might experience.

Genny, one of my clients who was devoted to her pets and to wildlife, was anxious to have a closer relationship with all animals. She told me that although she had practised telepathy with her pets, she was disappointed with the results, and asked for my help. I told her to pin a photograph of one of her pets to a door that she used all the time and, as she passed through it, to place her hand on the picture and silently ask her pet how it felt that day. Nothing happened for a week, but then, to her amazement, every time she carried out this procedure the animal started to talk to her. At first she thought she was imagining it, but the messages became clearer every day. She also had an overwhelming surge of well-being every time she received a message, almost as though the animal was giving her healing.

Then one day her whole body filled with dread, and she knew instinctively that something was wrong. The pet in question was a black and white spaniel called Mack. She noticed that he was rather quiet, and as she lay down on the floor beside him, he looked at her and she had the impression that he was telling her he was ill. When she examined him, she couldn't find anything that would suggest he was sick in any way, but she used her gut instinct and took him to the vet. He told her that Mack had a rupture in the groin which must be dealt with straight away. He was operated on that same evening.

When Mack was able to return home, Genny used silent thought to tell him how much she loved him, and reassured him that he would soon be well again. She noticed that whenever she made this contact, he would turn around and stare into her eyes. Eventually the impressions she received from him were so accurate that she realised she was actually having real telepathic conversations. When Mack recovered, Genny decided to pin photographs of *all* her pets on the door.

The only one that didn't seem to respond in any way was her cat Maggie, but this didn't surprise Genny in the least. She told me that the cat had always had a mind of her own and that she could actually feel Maggie closing her mind whenever she tried to link in with her.

However, on retiring to bed one evening, she woke

with a start and the feeling that her cat was ill. At first she thought it had been a dream, but decided to get up and investigate. She found the cat in the kitchen. She was being sick and was obviously in a lot of pain. When the vet examined her early the next morning, he told Genny that she had been poisoned, and immediately put the cat on a drip. Genny knew that some kind of thought transference between herself and Maggie had caused her to wake that night.

An acquaintance of mine experienced an entirely different form of thought transference. The lady in question owned a beautiful golden retriever called Henry. When they were out walking together she talked to him all the time. She admits that she found talking aloud cured her stress, but what she hadn't taken into consideration was the fact that the dog was picking up her thoughts.

One particularly cold and windy day, she was climbing a hill when she distinctly heard the dog tell her to return home. At first she thought someone had walked up behind her, but when she looked around there was no one in sight. Then she heard it again, and the dog grabbed the bottom of her coat and pulled her back. It was obvious at this point that Henry was very distressed. She ran back along the path, and as she approached her home she saw black smoke coming from the direction of the kitchen window. Pulling a scarf over her head, she let herself into the house – and found that she had left a chip pan near a flame and it had caught fire.

She called the fire brigade, and they managed to save half of the kitchen furniture. If she had not acted on the message she'd received from her dog, she would have lost everything. From that moment on she vowed that not only would she continue to talk to Henry, but she'd listen to what he had to say.

I have heard hundreds of stories of animals saving the lives of humans and of their own kind. In the telepathic world in which they operate, the mind is free, and will immediately respond to energies that contain negative vibrations. Then they interpret them. The reaction to this process is extremely rapid.

Never underestimate any creature's telepathic abilities; different species not only have their own language but through energy channels can also inter-pret the language of others. There can be no greater example of this than the healing given to humans through swimming with dolphins. There have also been stories of humans being picked up by dolphins and safely deposited on the beach after a shipwreck.

The more we learn about other forms of life and their remarkable feats, the more we are forced to look at our own shortcomings. We should treat all life with greater respect. Thinking about taking action is useless, though – there is far too much thought, and too little faith, to put these ideas into practice. It is only faith in our own potential that can break down barriers, because proof of that potential comes after the act and not before.

It is also exciting when you become involved with a project which is never ending. Communication with animals becomes a life-time hobby, and keeps you in touch with nature all through your life. There is no better teacher, for nature is changing all the time. The changes that come with the seasons of the year are no different from the seasons of our own lives, and nature can help us make the transitions for a better future.

So many gods, so many creeds,
So many paths that wind and wind,
While just the art of being kind
Is all the sad world needs.

The World's Need
Ella Wheeler Wilcox
1855–1919

CHAPTER 7

Animal Mind Magic

I have been healing animals all my life. As a professional healer over a period of thirty years, I have been able to observe, diagnose and heal thousands of animals worldwide.

From the many letters I have received, it has become apparent that the three greatest gifts I've been given are the secret of self-healing, an understanding of distant healing, and a spiritual philosophy which everyone can follow because of its simplicity. Without this knowledge, sick people all around the world would feel completely isolated. With it, however, they have been able to heal themselves, their friends and families, and their animals. I think the following letters will inspire those of you who want not only to communicate with your pets but also to heal them.

The first letter is from Australia:

My name is Petra, and I have a sheep dog named Bertie. As we live on a sheep farm and have thousands of sheep to care for, you can imagine how valuable Bertie is to my husband and myself. He has been our constant companion and work dog for four years.

Then, four months ago, he fell ill. Although he had the best treatment that we could afford, no one was able to help because they could not diagnose the problem.

I had already collected some of your books so I decided to read them again, this time paying more attention to your tuition. Then I gave Bertie some healing. Although he obviously enjoyed the experience, nothing happened for a week. Then on the eighth day, he woke up, and dashed up and down like a puppy. We were amazed, but even more so when he ran outside with me quite prepared to follow my horse as I set off to work.

My brother managed to keep him inside for a day, but after that he resumed his duties and has never looked back.

It was a miracle, because he had been ill for so long, and we had nearly given up hope that he would recover. We still do not know what was wrong with him. But I now believe that with enough love and compassion we all have the gift.

The next letter was sent from South America:

I am a divorcee, and I have six children. I also have three dogs, so life can be pretty hectic at times.

A handyman looks after the house and land, and he is a great help to me. He is also very good with the children.

Unfortunately, one of the dogs, a German Shepherd, took a sudden dislike to him, which made life difficult. I loved the dog too much to have him put down, but I couldn't afford to lose my helper. On the day that I finally gave in and agreed to have him put down, a flash of light passed in front of me and I was given a mental picture of you. Obviously someone was trying to tell me something, but I had no idea what it could be. The experience unnerved me so much that I cancelled the appointment with the vet and went straight to the bookshelf where I keep all of your books. On looking through them, I saw a photograph on the cover of your first book, *Mind to Mind*, which was the exact replica of the picture I had been given. I held the book in my hands and looked at your face. As I did so, your eyes shone as though there was a light behind them. Looking straight into your eyes, I asked for help. I certainly wasn't expecting a miracle to happen, but I thought it might help if I carried your book around with me all day.

When I went to bed, I put it under my pillow and repeated my prayer over and over again.

The next day, my handyman arrived for work. He let the dogs out of their pen except the German Shepherd. Then something happened that both startled and excited him. Before he could shut the gate, the dog had jumped up and licked his face, and then started to nuzzle him. Listening to his story, I knew that my prayers had been answered.

That was a year ago, and the dog and the handyman are now inseparable.

I thought miracles only happened to other people, but this was mine, and I will treasure the memory of it all my life.

I have been told many times that people have been cured either by looking at my photograph or by holding one of my books. But this story was unique because of the blinding flash of light that appeared before the photograph. I think I can safely say that this was spirit intervention because of the deep love the woman had for her dog.

Although at times we may believe that our loving actions are not appreciated, I can assure you that every word and action is being recorded in another dimension. Sometimes the rewards for our good deeds are priceless.

I have spent decades teaching spiritual values,

but the biggest problems in our society are the people who, because of their own lack of gifts, constantly belittle healing and mediumship. When it involves discussions about the paranormal, the ensuing attacks and counterattacks are endless, especially in television programmes. Fortunately, I have not had to suffer this kind of madness, because I've always refused to take part in these nonsensical programmes. To date, I have never had an offer to take part in a one-on-one television interview. It seems there always has to be a studio audience and opposing practitioners present, which can result in mayhem. How on earth is one supposed to discuss such important issues in this kind of atmosphere?

I write books because this way I can teach, and as they are sold worldwide I feel that I am filling a gap that needs attention. Because of their complexities, the gifts I have are particularly difficult to teach to the general public. One example is the way I am used as a channel so that energies can be mixed and matched for healing; another is how the mind of the person who wishes to communicate with me attaches itself to *my* mind in order to send telepathic messages of survival.

These phenomena are particularly difficult to explain because they are never the same. Real magic can never be analysed without losing its beauty and power. Sometimes I am told when a miracle is imminent, but this is a rare occurrence.

If you look at a beautiful flower, it will fill you with wonder, but if you pull it apart, you will have destroyed the beauty, the wonder and the magic of the moment, and will be left with nothing. The same is true of psychic phenomena – unless we accept the whole, we will never understand real magic.

If someone is genuinely interested in studying the paranormal, they will find a teacher of good repute. When they have carefully studied the subject for a number of years, *then* they can criticise – but not before they know what they are talking about.

However, it seems that sometimes television does have its uses, as you will see from the next story.

My name is Ian, and I am a university student. I have a bitch called Cherry who used to pine every time I left home to return to go to university. Although my mother has a lot of patience, the dog's whining often reduced her to tears.

Then one day, whilst she was watching a video of our last holiday, she noticed that every time I came on the screen, Cherry was entranced.

The next day, my mother took a photograph of me to a chemist and had it enlarged. She then attached it to the television screen with a piece of sellotape, so that the photograph could be folded back out of the way when the television was on. From that day on Cherry changed. There was no more whining. But every night she waits for my mother to pull the photograph down on to the screen before she goes to sleep.

If Ian had carried a photograph of Cherry around with him and mentally reassured her, she would have received his vibrations, and this could have worked just as well. Distant healing is all based on telepathy. The messages are received not only in this world but in other dimensions too, so you get the best of all worlds!

I have had excellent results with distant healing for treating depressed animals. In fact it is the best way to deal with depression, because it can be given several times a day. Although depression is an accepted illness in humans, it is a condition that people rarely recognise in their pets.

Rita sent me this letter.

I have a Collie bitch called Annie, who was devoted to my husband. Unfortunately he died five months ago and she has been in a depressed state ever since. I sit for hours trying to encourage her to eat, but she refuses most of the food and is getting thinner by the day.

She has had medication for the condition, but it has only made matters worse.

I have enclosed a photograph of Annie. Please help.

I held the photograph in my hand and then made telepathic contact with Annie. It was immediately obvious that Annie was extremely depressed. It was difficult to ascertain her level of vital energy as it was so low. I talked to her three times a day, and on the third day I received a response.

According to the dog, Rita had given most of her husband's clothes away, and Annie missed the reassurance his scent gave her.

When I told Rita about the telepathic message I had received, she was shocked, as she had no idea that communication was possible, let alone that it could be so accurate. I advised her to find a piece of clothing that had belonged to her husband and place it in the dog's basket.

A week later, I received a call to say that she had found a coat and hat that he'd always worn when he walked the dog. These had been placed in Annie's basket, and she was back to normal. She had even begun to gain weight again.

The intelligence of the animal kingdom is under-rated. Birds and beasts are always expected to comply with our rules and regulations, but what about the majority which have a free spirit? Allow them to show you how to enjoy life. Give them the space to strengthen their minds so that a more powerful telepathic contact can be established. It may be difficult at first, but if you can reach them in this way they will eventually become more obedient. On no account should an animal be beaten or abused in any way, because it will be your enemy for ever. They never forget.

I used to have a small black bitch called Smoky. One day, when she was in season, she jumped a five-foot fence, but as she was about to run off I called her back. As she sheepishly walked back to me, she passed an old man with a stick. Without warning, he hit her over the back several times. She screamed with pain.

I took Smoky to the veterinary clinic to be x-rayed, and although her spine was intact, she had suffered severe bruising. From that time on, she could not be trusted not to attack anyone with a stick of any kind. It made life difficult for both of us, as I always had to find an isolated place to exercise her.

The incident taught me a lesson I never forgot, and throughout my life I have never once harmed an animal.

My mother was a follower of that great healer Harry Edwards and had received some wonderful healing from him, so she suggested that I should write to him and ask for healing for Smoky. I agreed to do this, but it didn't help at all. If I had known then what I know now, *I* could have helped her. But I was only in my teens at that time and had never heard of telepathy.

Although I built many barriers to stop Smoky

getting out whenever she was in season, on one occasion she did manage to escape and consequently became pregnant.

When she was a month into her pregnancy, I found a large pedigree sheepdog sleeping in the porch of my home. I had no idea where he had come from, but assumed he was the expectant father. He was still there two days later, so I informed the police, and they looked after him until he was claimed by his owner – who then contacted me and asked me to let him know if the dog returned to me.

Months later, a few minutes after the birth of the pups, we found the sheepdog on the doorstep again. This time he had brought a present – the largest bone I had ever seen. As he lived three miles away, he must have set out on his journey whilst Smoky was in labour, to arrive at just the moment she gave birth.

I allowed him to see the new born pups before his owner arrived to take him back home. It was a magical experience, and one I have never forgotten. As the sheepdog walked away from the house, he looked a very proud dad indeed.

The emotions animals feel are no different from our own, but are too often dismissed by owners who simply do not understand them. These emotions are highlighted when the animals are left with strangers, or in kennels when their owners go away on holiday.

The next letter demonstrates the healing power of animals.

I have a Labrador dog with attitude. His name is Ben. Unlike my other Labradors, he is determined to go his own way and completely ignores commands. He seems to live in a world of his own. Sometimes I'm not sure whether this dog is for real, or whether I'm dealing with a spirit dog. He is really weird. At one time I was so fed up with him that I thought about sending him to another home, where he wouldn't be expected to work for his keep. But then one day everything changed.

One of my other dogs, Jasper, fell ill. The vets were unable to diagnose the problem, and although we tried every means within our knowledge to cure him, he was fading fast. I was in despair, and when I went to bed one night, I thought that he would not survive until the morning. I was so worried that I got up in the middle of the night to check on him – and to my amazement saw Ben snuggling up to Jasper, holding him with his front leg as though he was giving him a hug. Neither dog moved as I walked toward them. In fact they were so still that I thought Jasper was dead, but then I saw him move. For two days, apart from going out into the garden to relieve himself, Ben lay beside Jasper day and night. On the third day I walked into the room, and found them both sprinting around like puppies.

We never found out the cause of Jasper's illness, but I'm convinced that he owes his life to a very special healer.

Since then, Ben has healed not only other dogs, but cats, chickens and other livestock too. They all get the same treatment whenever they're poorly. He is a gem. He is still a free spirit, and is often 'away with the fairies', especially when he is expected to obey. He is different, and we love him for it. Now we wouldn't have him any other way.

I have heard many stories of animals who can heal. If you have such a pet, don't expect it to take direction, but if you look and listen you will learn a lot. These animals also have to be forgiven their sins, because they are completely unaware that they have committed any. Most of the time they live in a dimension that does not imprison, and that is where they prefer to live. I'd go along with that!

Move along these shades
In gentleness of heart; with gentle hand
Touch — for there is a spirit in the woods.

Nutting
William Wordsworth 1770–1850

CHAPTER 8

My World

I remember clearly the Sunday morning visits to my paternal grandmother and how she used to describe to me everything I had been doing that week. I thought this was magic, and in a way it was, for what can be more magical than communication with spirit entities?

Well, the ability to connect with the other species who share this planet is pretty magical. This is my world. I hope these stories will strengthen your own resolve to become closer to nature.

I was contacted by a lady who managed some stables. She was particularly worried about a horse called Tacky. When he was in the stables, he was fine, but as soon as someone tried to ride him he limped and refused to finish the ride.

He had been checked out at the veterinary hospital and had also been seen by a animal psychiatrist, but to no avail. The owner had apparently decided that if I couldn't do anything with him, Tacky was to be put down. There were many people who were devastated at the thought of this handsome creature losing his life over a problem they felt could be solved.

This gave me my first clue: lovable characters, human or beast, are usually great actors.

I was given a photograph of Tacky, and I began the healing process by looking into his eyes. This acts as a focus and frees the mind. I felt myself going into a daydreaming mode, where I was able to create a telepathic link with the horse. I was filled with sadness as I made the contact, and tears ran down my face. The message I received was that Tacky had originally belonged to a young girl, who had loved him dearly. For some reason he had been sold on, and although he was treated well at the stables, he'd lost the love that he had known all his life. He told me that his real name was Major, and that he hated his new name.

I spoke to him for some time, and assured him that I would do everything possible to help him, but that it would make things easier for everyone if he stopped his play-acting whenever he was taken out. I gave him healing, and finished the session.

You will notice that I did not *promise* Tacky that I could help him, and this is important. Never make promises unless you know for sure that you can fulfil them, because failure could make matters worse. The animal would feel, yet again, that it had been let down.

I called the manager of the stables and told her everything. To my surprise, she believed every word. She told me that there were certain animals with whom she had had telepathic conversations. Although at first she had thought they were things she was conjuring up in her own mind, she had eventually realised after many years of testing that this was not so. She had guessed that the lack of love had had something to do with Tacky's behaviour, even though he did receive some love every day. But she admitted that although she knew that horses do have lifetime attachments to certain people, it would never have occurred to her that a horse would become attached to a *name*. She assured me that she would make the owner aware of what had taken place.

The next call I received was to tell me that Tacky had been out several times and had behaved impeccably. The owner had been so upset when she heard the story that she now visited the horse twice a day and had shown it so much love that she now felt she had a special bond with it. And Tacky was now called Major again.

Thoughtlessness towards animals is one of the main causes of their bad behaviour. Having communicated with them all my life, I have learnt to respect

105

animals' intelligence and act accordingly, and they have always met me halfway. Telepathy is a language that breaks down all barriers.

One might think that Major's story was remarkable, but the sad fact is that such things can be all too common. Horses are beautiful, intelligent creatures and should be treated with dignity and common decency. But greed can override these basic needs.

We owe horses so much. Without them, civilisation as we know it would not exist – another reason why they should be treated with respect. Not so long ago they were our only means of transport. In many under-developed areas around the world, horses are still the only way to travel.

Another animal that is victimised on a regular basis in this country is the badger. The shocking stories and pictures of this abuse are constantly seen in the media, and yet the abuse goes on.

On one occasion I was asked to heal a wild badger that lived in a sett in someone's garden. Because badgers are retiring, nocturnal creatures, I thought this would be difficult, but I was assured that it would be easy enough because the security lights lit up the feeding area whenever the badger arrived. It came at the same time every night, and it loved fruit and cereal – especially if soaked in honey – so it was easy to tempt the creature.

The owner of the garden told me that she thought

the badger had damaged its right hind leg, though she didn't think it was broken. At the time I knew very little about badgers, so I rummaged through my nature books and found an appropriate picture of a superb specimen. That is how I wanted this badger to look. I studied the picture for two days, and then sent some healing to the injured animal. I did this by conjuring up a picture of it in my mind and directing a beam of energy to its hind leg. I did this every day for a week, and the healing worked. I was told that the animal no longer walked with a limp and seemed to be in good form.

The lady asked me what time of day I gave the healing, and when I told her that it was at 9.00 p.m. she laughed, and said, 'That's when the badger calls for its food, and I have noticed in the past week that it now turns around three times before it eats.' She had never seen it do this before. Months later she rang again to inform me that since the healing had stopped, the badger had stopped turning in circles.

I hope that the stories in this book will guide you and help to evaluate your own successes. I must remind those of you who genuinely want to have an interaction with the animal kingdom – and with nature in general – that you are not competing against anyone. Your experiences and progression will be unique to yourself. Until you have confidence in your own abilities, do not discuss your aims with anyone. Remember, you are moving into kingdoms that are strange and beautiful, and where magic is an everyday occurrence. The uninitiated cannot hope to be welcomed if they are constantly questioning every move. The secret is to *believe* that something can happen, and it will.

I have received thousands of letters from keen gardeners, who have been reduced to tears at the sight of molehills scattered about their lawns and their dying vegetables, the roots damaged by the moles tunnelling underground. Unfortunately, moles are especially difficult creatures to move on once they have found somewhere where they can indulge their passion for worms.

Through practice, however, I have found that each situation has to be treated differently. I begin by using my mediumistic abilities to scan the garden in question, paying particular attention to the surrounding area. If you have no developed psychic abilities ask the owners to give you a rough sketch of the garden which you can use as a focus. Then find a photograph of a mole and pin this on the sketch. Find a quiet place where you can study and absorb the pictures, then allow your mind to wander. Feel yourself being taken to the garden and then, with your mind, probe beneath the surface so that you can see the moles in the burrows. Talk to them.

Tell them that their lives are in danger, and that they will be safer if they move further afield. Try convincing them as though you were speaking to a wayward child. This exercise should initially take no longer than ten minutes. With practice it takes ten seconds. It may not work the first time, or even the second, but with perseverance you will succeed.

The exciting part of this exercise is that you are probing with your mind, becoming part of the Earth that feeds you, and it is another step forward in your quest. Understanding nature in all its forms is the most exciting thing that can happen to anyone.

My own experiences with moles have been successful. On one occasion I was asked to get rid of the moles on the lawn of a large estate. I had a mental picture of the place and thought at first that the problem would be too big for me to handle. But I quickly realised that I was conjuring up doubt, which is the most negative thought one can have in these circumstances as it closes the mind. Happily, this assignment turned out to be easier than I had thought, because there were so many acres that I could direct the moles to. The manager of the estate was delighted when they moved on two days later and were found to be inhabiting a field where their presence did not incur the wrath of the owner.

Moles can also be infuriating when they inhabit someone's greenhouse. One man rang me late at night, telling me that he was so angry at this intrusion into his beautiful greenhouse that he had stayed up night after night trying to shoot them. He had lost the fight, and in desperation asked me to help. I advised him to get a good night's sleep and reassured him that I would talk to the moles. He probably thought I was mad!

When I scanned the surrounding area, I found an ideal place for the moles to move to, a small field adjacent to a local pond. Apart from regular visits from a pet goat to keep the grass down, it was unspoilt. Through my psychic abilities, I was able to contact the moles in the greenhouse and ask them to leave, sending them a graphic picture of where they should go if they wanted to survive.

When animals receive any kind of negative energy, they react in the same way as they would do if they were being threatened physically. They do not necessarily receive the pictures sent, but they do get a feeling that all is not well in their world and that it would be a good idea to move away. After the warning, I repeatedly send them pictures of their new domain. I am not quite sure how they perceive these images, but I do know that 95 per cent of animals reach the recommended destinations, and the other five per cent choose their own new sites. In the case of the greenhouse moles, they moved on and the gardener was able to get back to his vegetables.

*　　*　　*

Another example of this type of migration came after someone sent me a photograph of a farmhouse in South Africa. Every evening the house was surrounded by wild dogs which came trying to kill the chickens. Even when the chickens were wired in at night, the dogs still tried to tear the fences down. The occupants of the house did everything possible to rid themselves of these pests. They told me that as soon as they shot one dog, another would take its place – and they would become even more vicious than before. As I read the letter, I had the answer. It is something I have seen time and time again: violence will beget violence.

I requested a large-scale map of the area and asked the owner to mark with a cross the place he thought the dogs would be happy and where food was plentiful. After I had received the marked map, I spent some time trying to create a link with these wild animals. When I felt that a link had been successful, I sent them a mental picture of the map and of where I would like them to go. I assured them that they would find food in that area and that they would be safe.

The owner of the house contacted me two weeks later to tell me that the dogs had disappeared. He was delighted. However, two months after that he had to pass the dogs' new location and decided to look out for them, but there were no signs that they were there. But when he had travelled another ten miles further along the track, he recognised at least six of the original dogs. He told me that wild dogs cover a large area, so he wasn't at all surprised. He confessed that he had been amazed by how quickly they had disappeared from his homestead after my initial contact.

To protect his property and livestock from further attacks, I suggested he paint a large picture of a wild dog, then put a red cross over it, and hang it on a post outside his house. He did this, and according to the letters he sent me for several years, the dogs never returned.

I learned this bit of magic from a real magician, and it works! The wonderful thing about magic is that no one knows *how* it really works, but if you have faith in your own abilities it is surprising how successful you can be.

Animals are always aware of the healing energies that are being absorbed by their bodies. Whenever I am giving hands-on healing to pets, they always sigh and go to sleep. Dogs who have visited my healing room in the past have continually nudged me for more after the healing session had ended – and have been very offended when they realised they had to leave!

Interacting with nature, in all its forms, is wonderful, and one should never underestimate the lessons we learn from these experiences.

Animals are such agreeable friends —
they ask no questions, they pass no criticisms.

Mr Gilfil's Love-Story
George Eliot 1819–1880

CHAPTER 9

Children and Their Pets

Nina was nine years old and had brought her pet hamster to me for healing. She told me that it had a lump on its back and that the animal doctor had told her that it could not be cured. She had often heard her mother talking about the benefits of healing and how wonderful she thought it was, so Nina had decided that was what she wanted for her pet.

I asked her to put the hamster into the palms of my hands. As I folded my hands around the little animal, I could feel the growth on its back. When I looked back at Nina I could see that she was close to tears, so I asked her to place her hands over mine as I asked for the tumour to be dispersed.

When the healing session had finished, I gave Nina appointments for the next five days. But before she left, she asked, 'Who were you speaking to when you asked for help?' I told her that someone was always listening and caring for us, especially when we are in trouble, and that all you had to do was ask.

As I spoke she looked around her. 'I didn't see anyone,' she said.

'Well, I did,' I replied. I placed my hands on her shoulders and told her that one day, when she least expected it, she would see a spirit.

These were not just words. I could tell that this little girl was psychic, and that she would eventually become a fine healer. I had known it as soon as she had placed her hands over mine, because my whole body was suffused with an energy that would have been too powerful for the child to contain had it not been directed from an outside source. Someone in the spirit world was waiting to nurture this very special talent. In order to strengthen her gift, I asked Nina to help me with the healing every time she arrived for the healing session.

On the third day, we noticed that the lump had reduced in size and the animal's eyes were brighter. No matter what the species, animal or human, there is no way that a veil can be drawn over the eyes – they truly are the windows of the soul. I believe children have a way of looking into the soul of their pets, because they are always looking into their eyes. When all is well, eyes shine brightly; when health deteriorates, they become dull. That is why I knew that the hamster would recover. Sure enough, by the end of the fifth session the tumour had disappeared.

When Nina and her pet visited me for the last

time, she told me that someone had appeared to her in a dream the previous night and told her that it was her love that had cured her pet. She looked at me and said, 'But it wasn't me, it was you.'

'No, it was you,' I replied. 'Because you love your pet so much you brought him here for help. Without that love, he would have died.' Her smile was all the thanks I needed.

Years later I met the girl's mother again, and she told me that Nina was living in New Zealand and had become a professional healer.

A young woman booked an appointment for a sitting. Her father was the first person to come through and communicate with her. He told her that her dog was ill, and that she should take him to the vet.

She looked at me in amazement. 'My dog isn't ill,' she said. 'He's so lively we have problems keeping him quiet.'

'If I were you I would take your father's advice,' I replied. 'When I receive a diagnosis in this way, it is never wrong.'

She agreed. As she was leaving, she turned to me and said, 'My son is disabled, and he loves that dog.'

Later that week, she rang me. Apparently, the vet had found something wrong with the animal's thyroid and had given him medication. She asked if the dog could have healing, and I told her to bring him along with her son.

The first half of the healing session was quite fraught. It was obvious that the dog was in overdrive. Then, without warning, he lay on his back, closed his eyes, and appeared to go into some kind of trance. The little boy thought his pet had died, and began to cry. When I had calmed him down, I saw a spirit form bending over the dog, seemingly performing some kind of operation. When it disappeared, the dog gradually came to his senses, but was still very quiet when he left to go home.

Two weeks later, the young woman called me again. Apparently, when she had taken the dog for a check-up, the vet could find nothing wrong with him and had stopped the medication. The dog was also much calmer now and was apparently 'a joy to have around'.

The bonus was that the little boy also recovered from his crippling illness. The healing that had taken place in my room had enabled his own body to regenerate. Apparently he was so fascinated by the healing process that he insisted on giving his mother and the dog regular 'healing sessions' – whether they liked it or not!

When children are touched in this manner, they become loving and compassionate human beings, and that is a huge bonus.

George was eight years old and had suffered with chronic asthma from the age of two. When he came to me for healing, his mother told me that he cried himself to sleep every night because he wanted a cat. But because of his condition, his parents knew that his dream would never come true. However, while I was healing him, I had a vision of someone handing George a black and white cat, and I knew then that he would be cured.

I thought it kinder not to say anything at that point, but I did ask them if anyone in their family owned a cat. George told me that his grandmother, who lived nearby, had a tabby cat. With this information I was able to formulate a plan, and after five healing sessions suggested that they take George to his grandmother's house so that he could stroke the cat. His mother was shocked by this suggestion, but I asked her to trust me.

On his first visit, George apparently stroked the cat several times. His mother was extremely apprehensive and waited for a violent asthmatic reaction, but it didn't materialise. I suggested they repeat the exercise twice a week, staying a little longer each time. It was a huge success.

Six months later, George came to see me – carrying a cat basket. Inside was a black and white cat. I had not mentioned my vision to him or his mother. The joy on this little boy's face as he held his pet told its own story. I watched George grow up over the years, and he never suffered from asthma again.

*　　*　　*

Healing should be taught in every school worldwide, and especially in countries where medical help is scarce. It is a gift that everyone possesses, but like all skills it will wither if it is not used on a regular basis. Everything in life has to be nurtured if it is to survive, and in this respect the healing gift is no different to any other talent. Like a violinist, a professional healer has to fine-tune his instrument — the mind — to enable him to give his best at all times.

If healing became part of the school curriculum, there would be less drug and alcohol abuse and more compassion, because children would have been shown a positive path — a path that would lead them away from the excesses of today and make them useful members of our society. Closed minds are responsible for the kind of world that we live in today. The situation has to change.

Children take to healing like ducks to water. They have no hang-ups about whether or not they can heal, they just *know* that they can, and therein lies their power. They have no self-doubt. It is the one thing that people in every corner of the earth can practise. All you need are your hands. Compassion will follow.

Frederick was seven years old and had a pet canary that he wanted me to heal. His mother told me that she thought the bird was going to die and that she was having nightmares about the situation because her son loved the canary so much.

Frederick, his mother and the canary duly arrived for their first appointment. To their horror, I opened the cage, gently took the bird out and held it in my hands. The little boy protested that the canary would fly away, but I reassured him and told him that it wouldn't move. The healing lasted for about fifteen minutes, and then I placed the bird back in its cage.

'How did you know it wouldn't fly away?' the little boy asked.

'Because I have held many birds, and they know they're in safe hands.'

Frederick looked puzzled. 'So is it going to get better?' he asked. I said that I knew that it would.

They came to see me again the next day. The canary looked extremely healthy and was chirping away. Both Frederick and his mother hugged me. They were delighted with the outcome.

A year later I met the boy's mother again. She told me that their cat had been ill, and that Frederick had given it healing and it had recovered. She laughed as she said, 'Do you know what he told me? He said, "Betty knew the canary was going to live and it did." And he knew that the cat was going to get better.'

Frederick used the 'knowing factor' throughout

his life, finally becoming a successful game warden in Africa, where he used it to great advantage.

Every time children came to me with a pet, I taught them how to heal. By the time they left they were all convinced that they could do it. I also taught them that animals needed to see both a vet and a healer, as one looks after the body and the other the energy system. That way they would have the best of both worlds.

But pets die. This will probably be a child's first experience of death, and it has a devastating effect upon them – especially when they realise that nothing can be done about it.

Grace was eleven years old and had lost her cat. Her mother asked me to talk to her. When we met, I told her that it was only the body that had died and that her pet's spirit would remain close to her until she felt able to let it go, when it would join other animals in another place. At last, it would be a free spirit. I told her, 'If you allow it to go, with happy thoughts and memories, it will return when you least expect it.'

The little girl asked a lot of questions, and by the time she left she seemed to be more at ease with the idea of death.

Six months later her mother rang to tell me that one night Grace had been woken up by a cat jumping on her bed. When it nuzzled up to her face, she knew it was her cat; it had done this with her ever since it was a kitten. Then a stream of light lit up the room and Grace could see the cat's face. She started to stroke it, and she told her mother that the fur felt exactly the same as it had when the cat had been alive. When her mother asked how long the animal had stayed, Grace said she thought it was about ten minutes.

When you are in a trance-like state, as Grace had been, you are between two worlds, and time does not exist. Therefore it is impossible to make a judgement on how much time has really passed. When I have been giving trance healing, I have often had the feeling that I have been away for a week, when in fact it has only been half an hour.

Grace's mother was full of apologies when she explained that the child had admitted to her that she hadn't believed a word I'd told her on her previous visit. 'Grace believes it all now, though!' her mother laughed. 'She also told me that she would have been afraid if you hadn't already told her about the spirits. For that alone we would both like to thank you from the bottom of our hearts. Betty, you have opened doors that would still be closed if we had not met you.'

There are so many doors that are left closed because of apathy and ignorance. This is a tragedy, because behind each one there are visions which will not only enhance our lives but from which we can receive inspiration. I often wonder, what kind of a world do those people live in who are not spiritually inspired? Spirituality is the most beautiful of all gifts and cannot be compared to materialistic gains, which are shallow and blot out the depths of compassion and understanding that feed the spirit. First and foremost, we are spirit. The essence that feeds the physical is the real power. It does not deteriorate with age, nor does it depend on earthly things for its survival.

I have known talented people, specialists in their chosen careers, who have spent years perfecting their talents until they have found the most simplest way of using their particular gifts. The time spent on their projects was repaid tenfold.

To ensure the ongoing health of this planet we have to reduce everything to its simplest form.

But the poor dog, in life the firmest friend,
The first to welcome, foremost to defend.

Inscription on a Newfoundland Dog
Lord Byron 1788–1824

CHAPTER 10

Animals' Humanity to Man

Little is known about the bravery of animals who accompany their trainers when they enter war zones around the world. These animals have no choice. They are selected for their particular attributes and go through a rigorous and demanding training, after which some are discarded or put to sleep whilst others go on to play an important part in the danger-ous missions ahead.

Men and women in the armed services know the sacrifices animals have made to protect them in diffi-cult circumstances, but this is rarely brought to the attention of the general public. Animals of war share the lives of those they have been trained to protect at the expense of their own lives. The love between man and beast under these circumstances is a bonus and invariably creates a telepathic link that can never be broken.

Birds have also been used to save lives. During the war, carrier pigeons were used as couriers and sent into enemy territory. Thousands lost their lives, but for those who did return there were no resounding trumpets or honours.

Neither were there any honours accorded to the trainers, who gave all of their time and energy to the training programme, knowing full well that they were sending their precious cargoes on missions that would probably save other lives but end their own. The enemy had been instructed to shoot every pigeon that seemed to be on a mission.

But where are the statues honouring a trainer and his pigeons? I have never seen one.

So many creatures have been used as weapons in wartime and in peace, yet their worth has been forgotten. But those involved in their demise appear to have no shame or guilt when deciding who or what should die at the end of their mission. Many heart-broken soldiers have had to return home without their dogs, due to red tape. Each and every one of us should at least give them an occasional thought.

Although men have created circumstances which have led to the sickening destruction of human life from the beginning of time, this happens not only in wartime conditions but on a day-to-day basis in ordinary communities. It is in this field that police dogs excel. It would be a step in the right direction if more could be heard of their heroic deeds. At the very least it would educate the young and encourage them to be more compassionate towards all forms of life. There are still far too many young children who torture animals and think of them as lesser beings.

Animals, on the other hand, rarely kill unless they are hungry or unless they have been forced to live a desperate, unnatural life by the ongoing destruction of our planet. There are valuable lessons to be learnt here.

In today's climate, animals have no choice but to adjust to an environment which has been poisoned and degraded by senseless acts that booster the bank rolls of those maladjusted and ignorant entrepreneurs who believe that all life is dispensable. Our newspapers contain pictures and stories of famous people, most of whom would not be famous but for the fact that they have somehow acquired enough money to warrant recognition. They are part and parcel of an outdated system that divides them from the rest of society and which encourages the young to spend their time trying to emulate them.

It would be a far better world if the pages of our newspapers included stories and pictures of outstanding courage and heroic acts performed by animals, which so many people think are inferior to the human race. Time and again you hear someone described as an animal, when they have been cruel. This is not only unfair but untrue. Animals are more caring, devoted, accepting, non-critical and loving than most humans.

There are very few people in this world who are

not touched by the sight of newborn animals but when these creatures need protection and time, many turn their backs and walk away.

I want to end this section of the book with the following stories, collected during my travels at home and abroad. I hope they will help people to see animals in a different light and perhaps learn something from them.

A young Australian woman had bought her daughter Emmie a brown and white pony for her fifth birthday. As the little girl had been riding ponies for two years, her mother felt that she was now capable of having one of her own.

It was love at first sight for both of them. Emmie called the pony Smiley, because when he whinnied it looked as though he was smiling.

Emmie spent all her spare time grooming the pony and having what seemed to be telepathic conversations with it. They were inseparable.

Then one day, when they were out riding, the pony suddenly halted and stood stock still. No amount of persuasion by its small owner could make it budge.

Emmie's mother, who was riding her own horse, tried to jolly the pony into action, but without success. She jumped off her horse and investigated the ground in front of the pony. There appeared to be nothing wrong at all, but as a precaution, and knowing that horses have special instincts, she asked Emmie to dismount. They left the pony on its own, and a few minutes later it reared and appeared to jump over an invisible hurdle. When it landed on the ground it stood still, as though waiting for Emmie to ride again. Mystified by this behaviour, they returned home.

Because Emmie's parents felt uneasy, they made the decision to avoid that particular area in future. A few days after the event, however, a neighbour told them that a huge hole had appeared in the field, revealing an old mine shaft that was thought to be at least 300 feet deep.

Visiting the field, they found that the hole had appeared at exactly the same spot where Smiley had stopped. He had protected Emmie by refusing to move, and had jumped the space rather than go round it, pinpointing the dangerous area so that they could avoid it in the future.

Some people think horses and ponies are stupid. I don't think so!

Jack was ten years old and lived in New Zealand. He had been riding horses all his life, as this was the only way his family could oversee their many acres.

When he was eight, Jack decided to investigate an area that had always intrigued him, even though his father had forbidden him to go there. Reaching a rocky outcrop, Jack dismounted, and tried to walk on with the horse, but it wouldn't move. He tried to walk alone, but the horse barred his way. Everywhere he turned, the horse was there – it just wouldn't let him take another step. At last he sensed that something was wrong and turned back.

It was not long before Jack came across his father riding like fury towards him, and he knew that he was in trouble for disobeying his orders. But instead of the usual clip around the ear, he was hugged as though he'd been away for a year.

Later, his father told him about the outcrop. It was so dangerous that many people had lost their lives there. Some of the bodies had never been recovered. Because of the mysterious mists that blanketed the area from time to time, local people thought the place had been cursed. Although many warning signs had been placed around the area, they were often ignored.

In this instance, the horse had clearly done everything it could to save the life of its young owner.

When I was living in Spain, I spent many hours sitting on the beach, listening to the waves crashing against the rocks.

On one particularly breezy day, I saw a small dog looking out to sea and barking like mad. At first I thought it was barking at the waves, but it started to run back and forth between the sea and a young couple who were spreading towels on the sand. When they looked up, the young woman screamed and ran into the waves towards a small figure who nobody had noticed was in difficulty. She emerged with the child in her arms and went immediately to the nearest hospital. Fortunately the child survived its watery ordeal.

The extraordinary part of this story is the fact that the dog was a stray. There were dozens of people on the beach that day, yet the dog seemed to know that the child belonged to that particular couple.

There is a happy ending to this story. Following the safe rescue, the dog was eventually adopted by the couple and became the child's devoted companion.

This story was told to me by an ex-soldier who had been a dog handler in the armed forces. Whilst he was serving abroad, he found himself in a particularly dangerous situation. His platoon were making their way through a jungle, taking one step at a time through the minefields that had been laid by the opposing forces.

His dog Jack, an Alsatian cross, was the first in line. Whenever he sensed danger he would stand stock still, then the soldiers would investigate, and if they found a mine they would disable it.

But one day, Jack stopped and appeared rooted to the ground. As far as the platoon could see there were no mines and no immediate danger, but nothing would budge him. Because the dog had saved their lives on numerous occasions, the soldiers decided to lay low and see what happened.

Fifteen minutes later, an enemy patrol walked right past them. If the platoon had continued to press on, they would surely have walked into an ambush. Amazingly, Jack's intuition had saved them all.

Reggie was ten years old and prone to epileptic seizures, and his mother was naturally very protective of him. Eventually, though, he grew irritated by her constant supervision and became difficult to handle. His mother called and asked me if I could help, not only with Reggie's fits but with his general behaviour too. I agreed to see them a week later.

When they arrived I immediately sensed the antagonism that the boy felt towards his mother, so I took her aside and asked her to sit in an adjacent room whilst I gave the child healing.

Throughout the healing Reggie was fine. He had no inhibitions and talked about every aspect of his life, including the fits. He was an extremely intelligent child.

For years I had studied the electro-magnetic field around the heads of people who suffered epileptic seizures, and I had found that some of the links of energy appeared to be missing. This would have the same effect as a defective fuse in the home – the lights go out.

As a healer, I could tell when someone was about to have a seizure because of the change in the electrical charges emanating from the patient. Because of my many years of studying animals, I also knew that a dog would immediately pick up these abnormal changes in the child before a seizure and could act as an effective early-warning system for impending attacks. I explained the situation to Reggie's mother, and she decided to go ahead and get a dog.

They bought a small terrier, and the boy and his dog soon became inseparable. Before an attack, the dog would become hyperactive and this alerted the boy to an imminent seizure. It worked so well that Reggie's mother was able to relax and give her son more space. This helped their relationship and his aggression disappeared. As frustration can actually exacerbate this type of malady, the calmer environment led to a reduction in Reggie's seizures. If someone feels that they are being imprisoned in any way, they will react violently until they have their freedom. Animals and humans are not so very different.

We continued with Reggie's healing, and after a year, the seizures stopped altogether.

I believe that there is one area in veterinary practices that could be improved, and that is to have a quiet room where the bereaved can sit until they feel strong enough to go home alone. To lose a pet, especially one who has shared your life for many years, is like having your heart cut out. Tears do not ease the pain, and the loss is as difficult to handle as that of a family member or a close friend. The agony is the same.

Although I have given solace to thousands of people after the death of their pets, they have still had to spend days and weeks alone, trying to come to terms with their loss, until they could see me.

I think the following quotation sums up the reason why pets have such a special place in our hearts.

I think I could turn and live with animals, they are so
placid and self-contained,
I stand and look at them long and long,
They do not sweat and whine about their condition,
They do not lie awake in the dark and weep for their sins,
They do not make me sick discussing their duty to God,
Not one is dissatisfied, not one demented with the mania
of owning things,
Not one kneels to another, nor to his kind that lived
thousands of years ago,
Not one is respectable or unhappy over the whole earth.

Song of the Open Road
Walt Whitman 1819–1892

PART TWO

Relationships

Let knowledge grow from more to more,
But more of reverence in us dwell;
That mind and soul, according well,
May make one music as before.

In Memoriam
Alfred, Lord Tennyson 1809–1892

CHAPTER 11

Our Relationships With Each Other

In the next four chapters, I am going to write about the many problems in relationships that I have heard about during my years as a medium and healer. I hope that some of these experiences may help those who are currently suffering from similar problems.

I have often been asked to write about relationships. Having healed, listened to and counselled thousands of people of both sexes, I knew what an emotional minefield I would be entering if I agreed to do this, so I decided to leave well alone until I had found the right format. I now believe that I have found it.

I am going to describe experiences that left such an emotional mark that the individuals concerned had begun to suffer from severe health problems. That is why they came to me, not only for ordinary healing but for psychological healing too. They needed to talk to someone who would listen.

When bad things happen within a family, children

suffer. And it doesn't end there. Violence begets violence, divorce begets divorce, and so on. This is called conditioning, where over time unacceptable behaviour becomes accepted. As these children grow up and have relationships of their own, many believe they can leave those relationships whenever they please, regardless of the heartbreak this may cause.

It is wrong to pin the blame on one individual. Many of these couples will have got married while they were still very young and immature, and their judgement was therefore impaired by lack of experience.

Those who haven't experienced the pain of divorce are sometimes smug and intolerant of those who have suffered in this way. But I have found that if you refuse to read the signs, it is never too late for something to go wrong. Those small things that irritate need to be addressed as soon as possible before they get out of hand.

It is virtually impossible to give advice unless you have a clear picture of the whole relationship, and that is why my mediumistic ability has enabled me to go where others feared to tread.

I hope that the events and experiences related in these chapters will help my readers gain an insight into the minds of both sexes. Just knowing that you are not alone and that there are others who are experiencing the same problems, every minute of every day, may inspire you to act sooner than you might otherwise have done to try to save your relationship. Forget pride. Love must come first.

Obviously there can be no single cure-all. Emotions and memories go too deep for that. However, positive thought stimulates the healing process, which lightens the burden – and that can only be a good thing. If nothing else, I hope that these chapters will bring to light what human beings do to each other.

Living a life that has a spiritual void has now been recognised as one of the reasons that people fail to reach their particular goals, no matter how talented they may be. Many people have the wrong attitude towards spirituality because they have no idea what it means. It is very simple. The greatest gift we are given when we enter this dimension is that of mind/soul energy. Although this energy is separate from the physical body, it works in conjunction with it all the time we are on this planet. When we die, it returns to the source. The way we conduct our lives determines what we will get out of it – if we follow a path where we respect the rights of every living thing on this planet, we will enhance the spiritual side of the mind/soul. That is spirituality. It has nothing to do with religion, but is a Universal happening.

Clearly, there is no chance that we can always be virtuous! For example, if we are trapped in a situation where there doesn't seem to be any means of escape, our aggression will come to the fore and, like animals, we will attack whatever is threatening us.

It is important to remember that no one can be right all the time. Humility can work wonders when all else fails. If you care about others, then you can't go far wrong.

People are shocked by the inhumane treatment of those who live in war zones. But similar things are happening all the time in ordinary homes throughout the world. Remarkably, many people manage to live their lives to the full without becoming bitter and twisted, in spite of how much they have suffered. Like nature itself, we are resilient, and most of us manage to retain some modicum of self-respect despite what has been done to us.

Most of us have regrets. But I hope the words that you will read in the following pages will help you to understand not only yourself, but others too. Perhaps they will also teach you something that is quickly going out of fashion – the art of listening.

The eye of man hath not heard,
the ear of man hath not seen,
man's hand is not able to taste,
his tongue to conceive, nor his heart to report,
what my dream was.

A Midsummer Night's Dream
William Shakespeare 1564–1616

CHAPTER 12

Relationships – For Women

In this chapter I shall be discussing relationship problems mainly from a woman's point of view – but men should also read this.

One of the main assets a healer needs is the ability to listen. People are often ill because they have no outlet for their frustrations. But if they had a good friend, someone they could trust and who would be prepared to listen to them from time to time, they wouldn't need the services of a counsellor.

The individuals in family units are becoming more and more isolated because the respect that used to exist within families is rapidly disappearing. We live in a world where time is of the essence; people want more freedom – of thought, word and deed – and they have to work hard to help pay for these things. And after working hard all day apart from each other, a family will probably spend their evenings silently watching television, with the result that parents often retire to bed still nurturing their unspoken doubts and irritations. This can eventually lead to depression and illness.

Children have the same problem. If they try to interrupt a programme their parents are watching they are either ignored or told to keep quiet, so they take their frustrations to bed with them. These habits do not make for a happy family.

The success of any long-standing relationship is based on mutual respect, on giving each other time and on listening. If this factor is missing, relationships can fall apart. If someone feels neglected, they will look elsewhere for comfort – and may eventually find a new partner who will give them the respect they believe they deserve.

Relationships are difficult. When you allow someone to enter your life, you are giving away a large slice of your freedom; and most of us like to be free spirits! I hope that this chapter will help enlighten you and possibly save a relationship that is in danger of slipping away. It should also help those who are starting to think about sharing their lives with a partner.

One of the main grudges I have heard voiced by women has been the complete inability of their partners to recognise when a relationship was in danger. The men invariably refused to discuss the issue and – even worse – pretended that it just wasn't happening.

'Is he deaf, dumb and blind?' the women would

say to me. Or, 'We seem to have nothing more to say to each other. It's over!' Tears would roll down their cheeks as they emptied their hearts of years of frustration.

A huge majority of these women had children, so leaving their partners was not an easy option. Instead they lived in an abyss of despair as their marriage deteriorated to such an extent that it became a living hell. Meanwhile, their children changed from happy outgoing kids to neurotic pawns, caught up in the psychological games their parents were playing out every day. No matter how much counselling the children received later, it could never make up for the damage that had been done in their young lives.

Fortunately, as a medium and a healer, I was able to access a full picture of the problems facing both partners and, with the whole of the family in mind, was able to give advice accordingly.

I would encourage the adults to take responsibility for their own lives, and in doing so, eventually take responsibility for their own actions. There is little chance of us always making the right decision, so you must be prepared to learn by experience.

I would also encourage them to allow their children to have their say, because 'out of the mouths of babes', the parents might learn something, especially if they had lost their own 'child within'. Because major decisions eventually affect each member of the family, all must be kept aware of what is happening. It is surprising how responsive even the youngest child can be when he or she is treated with respect. Involvement also makes things much easier as family members are less likely to continually blame each other for their disintegrating home life.

If the marriage cannot be retrieved, it is better to acknowledge that mistakes have been made and to try to lessen the inevitable pain and heartbreak. There are usually faults on both sides, but acknowledging them can be extremely difficult. Pride is involved, and both parties will want to attract the most sympathy from family and friends. But pride goes before a fall. No matter how bitter you may feel, life must go on, and looking towards a happier future will help you to remain positive. Your health depends on it!

Many people go through life blaming others for their mistakes. Behaviour like this can damage their reputation to such an extent that when they're in real trouble, they will be ignored. In a family situation, a character weakness like this affects everyone – including the children, who may adopt this kind of behaviour as a way out for when *they* are in trouble.

This can be exacerbated when both parents believe that their offspring are completely innocent of any misdemeanour known to man. It is even worse when one parent chastises a child for doing something wrong and the other parent is not supportive of this line. Children whose parents don't agree on what kind of punishment should fit the crime invariably grow up with misconceptions about who they are and where they are going. They will also play one parent off against another. Children are not as innocent as we would like to believe! They are small versions of every kind of personality one meets every day. They need discipline, loaded with love and understanding, but you'll never know whether you're on the right track if you're not prepared to listen to them. Children are human beings, and I have never yet met one who has been born to sainthood!

There is a desperate need in our society for parents to 'know' their children. When there are several children in a family, they will probably all be as different as chalk and cheese, and their needs will be different too. This is where the ability to listen to them as individuals will help maintain a happy environment for all. It is at this point that parents should encourage their offspring to be independent and teach them how to take on the mantle of self-responsibility. They can only do this by example.

It is impossible to expect everyone in a family to be pleasant at the same time. There will always be conflict of some kind. But when the family is in trouble, it will make things much easier if the children have learned from an early age that they must be supportive of each other during times of stress.

When relationships hit a bad patch, there are

plenty of people around ready to give advice, and this can be dangerous for everyone involved, because the very nature of a close relationship is one of secrecy. Thoughts and dreams are sacred, and people don't want to share them – not even with their closest friends. It is this secrecy that people share in the sanctity of their homes which very often prevents them from asking for help. If at some time either partner does seek help, however, then it must be given in a way that is not intrusive. They need to be able to talk without being judged. Those who are caught up in the turmoil of a bad relationship are often unable to make rational decisions. In fact, they shouldn't make *any* major decisions until they are able to rationalise their situation and explore all the alternatives.

Unloading heartbreak and grievances can be a major step forward for some people, but if they can do this in the company of a trusted friend it might prevent a complete mental and physical breakdown. Emotions run high and there has to be an outlet.

I have had many clients who wanted me to become emotionally involved in their unhappy marriages and divorce proceedings, but for a healer to take this path is akin to a civilian entering a war zone. Many thought that I ought to be 'on their side', and although this is understandable when someone is looking for support, it is not the kindest action.

There are always two sides to every story and it is only those who are directly involved who should be involved in the final analysis.

Instead, I was able to give these people healing, which calmed their troubled minds and introduced logic into an illogical situation. This was not as easy as it sounds. The last thing people want when they feel used and abused is logical thought. They want to be illogical, irrational, to rant and rave and vent their feelings on anyone – innocent or otherwise – who happens to be available.

Women who felt this way told me that they were furious when their men-folk walked away at a time when they needed them most. But men find it extremely difficult to listen to these tirades. They simply cannot handle it. They are different from women who, no matter how long it takes, will stand their ground until they have reached a satisfactory conclusion. A mother will always fight like a tiger for the preservation of her home and family, so the general reaction from these women was, 'My God! Here I was crumbled and broken, and he just ignored me.' So, no matter how difficult a man might find it, he should try to stay and listen. If not, it will be downhill all the way. A woman never forgets that when she needed her partner the most, he simply disappeared.

The question is, *why* do women want their partner to stay and listen to their screaming tirades? The answer is that they want their man to hurt as much as *they* are hurting. They need him to feel the same pain and humiliation that has dragged them down to that level.

It is particularly difficult for women whose partners leave home if they have no income of their own with which to pay the bills and maintain a secure home for their children. Resentment can lead to ill health, and women are especially prone to this when they are entirely dependent on the generosity of their ex-partner for all their needs.

This aspect of divorce can bring the worst kind of mental pain, so it is essential that you draw a line where you believe the humiliation should stop. It may be necessary to let go of an easy life and work towards an independent lifestyle. If you have the courage to do this, you will be the guardian of your own life and you can draw up a new blueprint that will inspire you to achieve what might seem to be an impossible dream.

In all relationships, honesty is the best policy. In the conversations I have had with my clients, I have found that what hurt them most were the lies. They have told me that if their partners had been honest and not put them through the mill with accusations and counterattacks, they would have recovered far quicker than they did once everything was finally brought to light. As it was, the end result was destructive to both parties. Some never spoke again, even though they shared the responsibility for their children.

It is much better if the guilty party can be courageous enough to tell the truth and take the consequences. If they allow their partner to express their feelings of hurt and anger, it will ease their pain. No one should have to go through this kind of hell alone – no matter how unpleasant it may be, they should listen to each other. It will go a long way to ridding themselves of dangerous blockages in the energy system and lessening the risk of a physical and mental breakdown.

It is worth remembering that somewhere along the line there was love and understanding between you, and what you loved about your partner will still be there beneath the surface. That is why rationally you should not want to cause more heartbreak and more grief. If someone is hurting you must try to help them.

Of course, there are a thousand and one ways of making life hell for other people, but don't let it be you who drives another human being to the brink. There are kinder ways of solving problems. In these situations, patience is a virtue.

I have heard some shocking stories, and having heard the full account from both parties I know that the outcome would often have been different if only they had sought outside help earlier. By the time they consulted me, the damage had been done, and it was often too late to save the relationship.

Another complaint that I have heard many times over the years is, 'He never tells me he loves me.' To men this may seem trivial, but never answer with, 'Of course I love you. *I married you, didn't I?*' These words bring out the worst in women. After all, the decision to marry is mutual, and – from what I have often been told – the woman's reply, silent or otherwise, is, 'Why does he think he's so special?' (Or something else quite unrepeatable!) In fact, many women have bitterly resented the fact that they were doing all the nurturing in the relationship. Some sort of loving response from their partner would have gone a long way to help the situation.

What also came to light over the years was the fact that men – young and old alike – seem to choose different partners to meet different needs. For example, young men often choose women who will make good mothers and housekeepers. They feel that this gives them an air of respectability in an adult world. But it is surely no coincidence that the word 'adult' is also the first part of the word 'adultery', for without continual mental and emotional stimulation, many men become bored and start having affairs.

Older men seem to look close to home for an affair. Wives can sometimes praise their friends to their husbands to such an extent that the men become attracted to these apparently saint-like individuals. 'I only praised her because he didn't like her,' one woman said. 'He used to make the most awful remarks after her visits, saying she was plain, dowdy and boring.' Many of the women confiding in me were attractive with delightful personalities, and I could understand their amazement when this infidelity happened to them.

On the other hand, plain-looking women often have very good marriages. Whether this is because their husbands feel safe with someone who is not being pursued by other men, or whether they believed that they had to compensate for something they felt was lacking within themselves, I do not know. Certainly, these less glamorous couples invariably seem to feel secure and protected in each other's presence.

I know there are hundreds of marriages which seem to have it all – handsome husband, attractive wife, wonderful children and a beautiful home. But I've listened to people who have this lifestyle, and I know that you cannot judge by appearances. Marriage is more complex than that.

'Trophy wives' seem to have become a phenomenon of modern society. Many male executives find that they want to change their old model for a new one, preferably someone half their age. This may be because they feel that their 'old' wife hasn't kept pace with their own needs, or it may be because they want to impress their associates. Some men don't go this far, but instead humiliate their partners until they change their image – the end result of which, of course, is that their wives will then look just the same as all the other 'trophies'. The fact that these men once thought that their wives were unique with wonderful personalities is apparently forgotten.

Unfortunately, the wives who obediently fall into this pattern open the door to a hell they could not have dreamed of. They will constantly have to spend time on their appearance – hair stylists, make-up, clothes and jewellery – as well as looking after their children and their home. This is not just my opinion, but that of hundreds of fatigued women who have asked for my help when they've eventually had to give up the fight.

We mustn't forget, however, that there are women executives who think along the same lines. They have their trophy men, the so-called 'toy boys'. True and honest relationships can be buried in the wheeling and dealing of the business world. The tragic end result is the death of a good relationship. In the future, there will be countless retired men and women who will long for a warm and lasting relationship once the need for those 'executive toys' has gone.

I often wonder why businessmen choose to spend time with younger women who cannot share their memories of the past? We know how frustrating it is for middle-aged people who mention a movie star or the like to their children who don't know whom they are talking about – it can make you feel really old! The same thoughts must go through the minds of men who are in a relationship with a much younger woman. Their memories are of no interest to young wives. Many of these women are only interested in the prestige they gain when seen on the arm of their lover.

It is extremely hard for the women who have been left behind, those who have cared for their children and sacrificed their own careers, only to find themselves alone, part-exchanged for a younger model. Unfortunately, there are no winners in a situation like this. No matter who is to blame for these unhappy relationships, in the end everyone has to pay a price.

So many times I have heard women say, 'Why has he done this? I thought we were going to spend our whole lives together.' Unfortunately, there is no simple answer to this question. The fact is that men and women are different. Their needs are different, and unfortunately experience and maturity don't always apply. Some women have retaliated by having an adulterous relationship of their own, but I found that many did not enjoy the experience. They would rather have a partner with whom they could relax and who is aware, after many years together, of their sexual needs and preferences. They told me that they found themselves in an empty place that was devoid of love, and I believe that to be the main difference between men and women. Men do not seem to need love – that extra ingredient – to be able to enjoy a sexual relationship. That is why, when they are found out in an affair, they rarely feel that they have done anything wrong.

Fortunately, a large proportion of women who have been left 'holding the baby' refuse to become victims and they reinvent themselves, often to the astonishment of their ex-husband. Some try to 'get even' through various means, but this will only exacerbate their heartbreak. It is much better to leave the past where it belongs and to become the architect of your own dreams and ambitions, and of a brighter future.

Many of the people who came to see me – both men and women – had realised that one of the main reasons for their infidelities was to lend an added zest to their marriage. I have always found this hard to understand. With a vivid imagination, they could have done exactly the same thing without looking outside their marital home. However, I also understand that it takes 'two to tango'.

Through these cases, it became clear to me that before anyone even thinks of starting a relationship, the couples involved should be completely open about their likes and dislikes, and about their sexual preferences – no matter how ridiculous or fanciful they may seem. It is during this time that any rejection of such things should take place, and not when the couple have become so close that airing them becomes an embarrassment to both parties. Make no mistake, if one partner is not satisfied with the sexual side of the partnership, they will eventually look for someone who can satisfy their needs. This is not a judgement, it is simply something I have learned over many years from clients and friends.

The constant battle between the sexes is also exacerbated by the hormonal problems that women have to cope with during their lives. Although some sail through life with no problems at all, others have to adjust as their mood swings back and forth. The worst time of all can be during the menopause. It is often at this time, when in fact they are most needed by their wives, that many men look around for a younger model. They no longer want to be seen with someone whose hair is turning grey, who has lines around her eyes and mouth, and who is often suffering from fatigue and depression. Menopause can be an uncomfortable and distressing time and at a time like this women need their partners more than ever.

The extraordinary thing I noticed about wives whose husbands had been having an affair is that they were able to forgive and forget providing they could place the blame of the adultery on the 'other woman'. If they can convince themselves that their man is the victim, they find it easier to forgive him and keep their home and family together.

Unfortunately, drawing a veil over your eyes in these circumstances is asking for trouble later, for the hurt never completely goes away.

There are always two sides to the story, but it is very rare that the wronged woman will even listen to the third person in the triangle, the so-called 'mistress'. If they did, they might find that they have much in common.

The few women I met who dealt with the situation in an intelligent manner – by putting the blame exactly where it belonged – managed to keep their marriage together. They insisted that everything, especially their husband's part in the affair, should be brought out into the open. That way they were assured that no more skeletons could suddenly pop out of the cupboard if they eventually managed to get their marriage back on track again. Rather than all the blame being put on the other woman, it was invariably shown that the man himself had done the pursuing, while an inexperienced young woman was often flattered by the attentions of a mature man, making herself easy prey.

I saw a great many of these betrayed women over the years as they came for regular healing, and the outcome of their stories was often fascinating. For example, about half of the women whose husbands had actually left the marital home to live with a mistress told me that their spouses soon begged forgiveness and asked to return. Having finally got what they wanted, neither the man nor his mistress found it as romantic as an illicit affair – and there is nothing worse than sharing one's home with an unwanted guest.

There may be times when a relationship can be strengthened after one of the partners has strayed. One woman told me that her husband had proved beyond any doubt that he loved her more now that she had aged than he did before. Another woman said, 'My husband loves the lines on my face because it reminds him of the various episodes in our lives when I earned them.' Her partner had accompanied her to the healing session, and when I jokingly asked him if this was true, he answered, 'Yes, she's right, because I put most of them there.' The positive conclusion to this partnership was down to the fact that the husband had changed in such a way that his wife had now found it in her heart to forgive him his trespasses. This proves that it is never too late to come to terms with the negative side of our character and reverse it. Why spend the latter years of your life alone when all you need for lasting happiness is a truthful and caring attitude? This couple had earned the right to the loving and comfortable relationship they will share in their last years together.

On one occasion a husband and wife visited me separately, both pouring their hearts out to me and confessing that they were having an affair – and saying that if their other half found out it would kill them! As they were both apparently having the time of their lives, I just let them talk until they felt better and left. I knew they would be back sooner or later; illicit relationships usually come to an end either because they die a natural death or because the guilty partner is found out or cannot resist spilling the beans.

I think both sexes generally underestimate the resilience of their partners, simply because having an illicit lover boosts their own ego to such an extent that they truly believe they are capable of holding down both relationships.

To have a successful long-standing relationship, it is necessary for both parties to be able to function independently of each other. The majority of marriages that break up fail because one partner has unnaturally high expectations of the other as far as love, happiness, success and a positive outlook are concerned. There is no doubt that such dependency is dangerous and will eventually reduce those involved to despair.

The same thing can happen when one partner is ill and has to rely on the other for constant care. There comes a time when carers must have a rest before they themselves become sick.

I have many friends who live separately from their partners to ensure that their lives will not be torn apart by the differences that can occur when people share a home. Those with children may try to live in a house that has separate rooms or flats. If this isn't possible, they will try to live close to each other so that their children can have a choice of homes and companionship. Although this type of relationship is unusual, there can often be more trust between the two partners than if they tried to live together. They are therefore able to create a more relaxed attitude within the family.

When they were questioned as to whether having so much freedom might be an excuse for having an affair, the couples involved said that if the relationship was that weak, they'd have an affair anyway, whether they lived together or apart. From their conversations, it was obvious that they all seemed to get satisfaction from having their own space. They took pleasure in making an effort to visit each other's homes, and this kind of excitement eliminated any need to seek a liaison elsewhere.

It is only possible to have this kind of relationship if the people concerned are mature and sure of their ground. Very few young people would pass this test! Others – who may be totally dependent or have a suspicious nature – would reject it. But what has become apparent to me over the years is the absolute necessity for everyone to have their own space. This can be incredibly difficult if you live in a small house or flat, but if there is a spare room, no matter how small, a rota can be drawn up so that each member of the family has some time to themselves when the rest of the family are denied access. This is an ideal arrangement if someone likes to study in private, browse websites on a computer, or simply sit and think in peace.

The world is changing faster than ever, and the old orders no longer apply. In the first half of the last century people getting married had to promise to love, honour and obey. Unfortunately, this seemed to apply only to the women; the majority of men worked hard, played hard and then expected their wives to wait on them day and night. No one seemed to give much thought to the mothers with large families who were expected to wash and iron every piece of clothing, slave over the meals, take care of the house and look after the children. By the time they reached the age of thirty, most of these women were already old.

Unfortunately, it is true that some people still live like this, possibly because of a lack of money, but most women now have a choice, especially when they have careers of their own. However, having those choices does not necessarily make life easier. In fact, decision-making in the emotional areas of our lives can become a curse rather than a blessing. The best way to deal with this is to bring the whole family in on the discussions; it will then be possible to see which members of the family will benefit from new ideas and who will be hurt. Compromise keeps everyone happy.

Not that life will ever be easy. You can bet that if one path looks easier than another, rocks will soon appear to block your progress until you find a solution. If you can accept this, you will be able to map your own journey. You will know from past experience that when you've made it over one hurdle, another will soon take its place. The bonus is that once you have solved one problem, you know that you are capable of tackling another. You begin to build up a blueprint which can be applied to all of the problem areas in your life.

Continually moaning about your circumstances is a waste of time and energy. Nothing will change until *you* find a way of changing it, and when you have found a solution, be strong enough to carry it through. So many people live in misery because they haven't the courage to change. What a waste of a life!

The most important thing to remember is that you must never attempt to solve your problems by trying to change other people. This is a mistake that the young often make before they marry or live together. Whatever your partner's character before you live together, that is how he will continue to be. 'I thought I could change him' is a phrase I have heard over and over again. Unfortunately, as you get older your partner's bad habits seem to get worse, and although age usually makes you more mellow, the irritations are always there.

Before couples commit themselves to a long-term relationship, they must accept their chosen partner for what he or she is. Even if your partner vows to change to try to please you, old habits and thoughts die hard, and resentment can be deep and bitter when someone has tried against his own instincts to change himself for the sake of peace.

We only learn wisdom through our failures, and wisdom is hard-earned. When I hear a few wise words being spoken, I know that although suffering has taken its toll, the speaker has learnt from her experiences.

An oft-repeated phrase from a divorced woman who visited me was, 'I want to move on, but I don't know how.' When I told her to live one day at a time, and to treat that day as though it were a miniature eternity, she told me that that was exactly what her life felt like – a never-ending day full of frustrations and tears. But she had missed the point – if you *live* one day at a time, you can't help but enjoy it as you put your heart and soul into pleasurable activities every single day. Within a month or two, a new excitement will enter your life as you sweep away the negative aspects of the past.

'Why has he done this? I thought we were going to spend our whole lives together,' is another complaint I have often heard. Unfortunately, there is no simple answer to this question. The fact is that men and women are different. Their needs are different. No matter how mature one becomes over the years, it doesn't alter this simple biological fact.

I have never met a woman yet who does not want to be loved. Love can make the difference between Life (with a capital 'L') and simple existence. We need to receive the outward expressions of love and the private closeness of another human being who wants to be a part of our life, someone who will regularly transport us to a place where the outside world does not exist. And yet talking to many women, I discovered that the majority of their partners seemed to be completely unaware that tender words and gestures are absolutely essential. But if women are expected to do all the chores in the home – as well as looking after the children, being a pleasing companion and a lover in bed – they will expect more from their partners, starting with tenderness and respect.

A large number of women have told me that, though they loved their partners, the financial problems they faced – such as paying mortgages and caring for their children – meant that one or both of them had to work incessantly to meet the demands. That was when love disappeared and anger and misery took its place. Certainly fatigue seemed to be a real problem for these women as they sought healing.

Of course the way to end this misery is to live a simpler life, but such a major change is not for the faint-hearted, nor for those who need the luxuries of life to sustain them.

One of the greatest pitfalls in life is high expectation, because reality nearly always falls far below that, and the result is an ongoing dissatisfaction with life. But there is a way out of this too – be happy and grateful for what you have got *at this moment*. If things improve, your excitement will be far greater than it would otherwise have been.

Healing always eased the burden of the women who came to see me, and I hope it will have given them the courage to find the answers to their problems. Time is also a great healer.

We come into this world alone, and we go out alone, and for a large part of our lives we are alone with our thoughts. If we are to survive, the answers have to come from within ourselves.

A good friend of mine, who is no longer here, always used to end a conversation with, 'Be kind to yourself.' This is great advice! So take note – don't let yourself down.

I've taken my fun where I've found it,
An' now I must pay for my fun,
For the more you 'ave known o' the others,
The less will you settle to one;
An' the end of it's sittin' and thinkin',
An' dreamin' Hell-fires to see.
So be warned by my lot (which I know you will not),
An' learn about women from me!

The Last Chantey
Rudyard Kipling 1865–1936

CHAPTER 13

Relationships – For Men

This chapter is mainly for men – but women should read it too.

I find it quite extraordinary, whenever the subject of healing is raised, that most people assume the vast majority of my clients are women. The truth is that over 45 per cent of my clients are men. I believe that the reason for this misconception comes from the men themselves. Perhaps they believe that their macho image would be damaged if they let it be known that they'd received healing.

Interestingly, this attitude is reversed if their children become sick. All self-consciousness disappears when the health of their child is at risk, and it is at these times that all prejudices are forgotten. The fact that someone near to them is in danger brings out the animal instinct. The lion roars – sometimes in anger, sometimes in despair.

I have heard numerous stories from fathers who, having shown this protective side whilst attending hospital with their sick children, were told to go away and pull themselves together. Good advice, but bad timing; for when someone close to them is in danger, they want to be with them, not locked out and alone. Besides, men are not very good at pulling themselves together at these times. Their hormonal makeup demands action, and they will not be able to relax. Only when they feel that they can safely leave the patient will they do so.

Once again, I repeat, men and women are different. But you can see *why* they have to be different. Quick action by the male in society stimulates a response. But once that has been achieved, it is the female who will soothe and bring things back to normal. One-parent families have to find a way of filling both roles, and this can be extremely difficult.

There is no doubt that a lot of men believe in healing, and it would help the cause of the healing profession if they could find the courage to admit it, if only to help someone else who is in a similar predicament. Women have no hang-ups at all with healing, and they discuss it openly with their friends, families and colleagues. There is no better way of pointing people in the right direction than by word of mouth. When men complain about the time women spend chatting, they should remember that words can move mountains!

It seems to me that the younger a man is, the more patience he has. Young men are often prepared to listen, but they have other problems to overcome. For example, young men are often completely baffled by the hormonal changes experienced by a woman during her monthly cycle. They continually complain about their partner's mood swings. Time and time again, they asked me what kind of mother a girlfriend would make if she couldn't control her moods and temper. Of course there was no answer to that particular question, because the problems are unique to each and every female. However, I was able to calm some of their fears by telling them that healing and alternative medicine can have a marked effect on the negative aspects of a hormonal cycle.

When I asked these men if their mothers had ever talked to them about women's problems, the answer was always no. It seems that a mother will talk to her daughter about sex, while the father talks to the son. No wonder there's so much ignorance about the hormonal make-up of both sexes! Frankly, I think both parents should have meaningful conversations with all their children. How else are young people expected to cope with the opposite sex if they're only ever given a one-sided view of a relationship?

Each sex employs different tactics when they are trying to attract someone, and learning this art can be a minefield in itself. Young men have often told me about a girl giving them the come-on all evening at a nightclub, yet shunning them when it was time to leave. When I explained that women had to be very careful if they thought they'd have to protect themselves from being taken advantage of, the men said, 'But surely that's what it is all about?' They just couldn't understand that the sexual needs of most females are not as rampant as those of young men! Also, a girl's parents will probably have warned her of the dangers of leaving alone with a man, especially as most rape attacks are perpetrated by someone who is known to the victim. They might even be plied with drugs so they lower their guard.

Since the sixties, there has been more sexual freedom than at any other time, but the truth is that women are still not free. There are no areas where a woman can walk freely without having to look behind her all the time. At one time women felt that they were protected if they took their dog with them on their walks, but this no longer seems to be the case. The dangers lurking outside the home are endless.

Men would attract far more women if only they could be more compassionate and understanding. Most women are fed up with the macho image, which these days is quickly losing its charm. One would think that men would be more compassionate the longer they've been married, but this isn't necessarily the case. 'My mother was a wonderful cook, and yet all my wife gives me are ready-made meals,' is a common cry. But in nearly all cases, these mothers never had a career and so had the luxury of time to prepare delicious meals. The wives on the other hand have careers in order to contribute towards the mortgage and other bills. Before men moan about the catering, they should sit down and think about it very carefully. Would they prefer financial help or home-cooked meals? If they treated their partner with a little love and respect, they might get both, perhaps at weekends. They might also like to cook for their wife occasionally!

Whilst discussing their problems, men sometimes confessed to me that they weren't *always* given ready-made meals but that they used this as an excuse to lead up to what was really troubling them. The term 'comfort eating' illustrates the importance that people put on food. It can be used as a solace if you're feeling depressed – and can also be used as a tool to inflict pain. Men consistently moaned to me about their wife's inability to give them the comfort foods they thought they were entitled to have. But it was never long before the true problems emerged – and these problems were nearly always sexually orientated.

In my opinion, these men should never have left their parents' home unless they were prepared to embrace a new set of rules.

It is the lack of courage in both sexes that creates an atmosphere of distrust, and this invariably leads to confusion and bitterness. Once it has become established, cutting through that bitterness is one of the most difficult tasks of all in a relationship.

However, it's a whole new ball game when children are involved. 'Why does she have to confront me with the children's problems as soon as I get home?' the men asked. 'All I want to do is to relax, but instead I get a running commentary about the kids. It drives me crazy.' It's a valid argument, and something women could think about. But it's a difficult nut to crack unless both sides are aware of the needs of the other. The mother has had to cope with the children all day without a break – there are very few children who do not need to be supervised every hour of the day. The mother can't take a leisurely bath or even have a minute in the loo alone until the kids are in bed. If they've been ill, or simply in a fractious mood, this takes an even bigger toll on her nervous system.

Men also have their daily burden. Their journey may involve a long commute, and when they get to work they have to spend the day pleasing other people. They take the same journey home at night. Feeling tired and sometimes dejected, they open the front door only to be confronted with a whole new set of problems to which they are expected to find an immediate solution.

Many men have told me that although they have tried to comfort their wife on these occasions, she will sometimes be too distraught to listen. This is when emotions run high, and one word out of place can lead to disaster. Again, it can be a good idea to provide comfort food before discussing the situation. Like horses, human beings are much more inclined to be compliant once they have been fed and watered.

When parents are facing this kind of dysfunction in their marriage, they have to understand that if the problem cannot be solved, the health of the whole family will be at stake. Having listened to children over the years, I have become painfully aware of the terrible traumas that they suffer whenever there is any kind of disturbance between their parents. They absorb the negative energy that is produced. This contaminates the atmosphere in their home, and exacerbates any damage to their young minds.

Most people want a peaceful existence. Yet men have told me that their greatest problem has been their wife's nagging – they simply cannot take it, and that is why they have to walk away. Nagging can become obsessive and is a problem that must be addressed before it gets out of hand. I have listened to both sides, however, and I believe that this situation is not one-sided – men can be dreadful nags too.

There is a way out of this predicament, and that is to put your thoughts down on paper, put it in an envelope, address it to your partner, and then place it where it will be seen. This way your partner can read the letter in private so that any anger they may feel will be diminished by the time the contents are discussed. Women who have used this method of communication have told me that it has actually saved their marriages. If it works, what a relief for the man who gets home at night and isn't greeted with tears and fears as soon as he walks through the door.

Men have often told me that their partner had a list of excuses whenever she wanted to opt out of sex, whereas she would be hurt and annoyed if the rejection came from the man – she saw it as a slight on their femininity. Worse still, a husband turning down sex seemed to spark off spasms of jealousy and accusations of adultery, which in most cases were completely unfounded.

There is a deep-rooted bitterness in many women, which stems from the fact that their partner will practically ignore them all day and yet expect them to respond to their sexual demands once they have gone to bed. Men would do well to note this grudge, because it will not go away. If they are kind, helpful and considerate throughout the day – with a spark of romance too – then they will be meeting their partners more than halfway.

Women hate to be ignored. It takes very little effort for a man to touch and hug, and it is a wonderful way for him to demonstrate that the bonding between the two is not just a means to an end but for him really does come from a genuine desire to be close to each other.

Although every relationship is always based around a question of give and take, there is no better way of bonding than to gain an understanding into what makes your partner tick. Every human being is unique, and each of us has different needs. This may appear unromantic at a time when romance is uppermost in your mind but this is not so. Exploring another person's potential is not only exciting but extremely sensual, and can draw two like-minded people together far quicker than the physical approach – that can come later.

Also, lust may take you down many different roads before you find the person you would like to spend your life with. It can be dangerous to judge someone by a previous partner – the past must be left behind when a new relationship begins or it may sour before it can be fully developed.

A lasting relationship has to be founded on a firm base, and it is important to establish some ground rules before taking it too far. Financial arrangements are often a bone of contention between the sexes. There are still many women who expect their men to pay all the bills and to keep them in a lifestyle they believe they're entitled to. This is another area where couples should put all their cards on the table before it is too late. Most men believe that if their partner has an income then she should be prepared to share the expenses.

Money is certainly the root of all evil within the home if the two people involved can't agree on how it should be spent. This always leads to disagreements and ultimately in many cases to divorce.

Sometimes a partner will leave the family home if he or she finds life intolerable. But the biggest problem arises when a third party is involved who is completely unaware of a new partner's married state. When the adultery is found out, the blame tends to be placed on the innocent party rather than on the one who conveniently forgot to mention the spouse to the new lover.

It is never wise to apportion blame. Everyone has secrets that cannot be shared, and these secrets may act as our lifeline when things go wrong. What others believe to be the reality of a situation may be very far from the truth. The only thing you can be sure of is that someone is going to get hurt. If the parties involved can minimise this by being completely honest and supportive to everyone – no matter how difficult this is – the final solution, no matter how imperfect, will lessen the pain.

I know this works because I have seen the results. It may not be a perfect solution, but it does mean that everyone involved can retain some self-respect. I have listened to enough case histories to know that when the worst is over, people often feel humiliated by the way they handled the situation. To 'keep your head when all about you are losing theirs' is something to be proud of.

For a lasting relationship, both sexes must 'know themselves' – the good and the bad. Talk to each other and *listen*. Not listening usually seems to be the main reason for the breakdown of a relationship.

When it happens, one way of reducing your partner's anger is to ask them to describe the different levels of frustration that have brought them to this point. It takes time, but there is often a pattern, and once that is recognised it will be possible for both parties to avoid that particular path again. Anger inevitably leads to isolation, and there is no gain in a lonely place.

Many people try to find solace in solitude, and although some succeed – for a while at least – cutting yourself off from the rest of humankind is a mistake. We are all a living mass of energy, and energy gains strength when it is interactive. That is why so many lonely people find that they simply get too tired to cope with normal life.

Men have always used pubs and clubs as a means of relieving stress, but this provides only a temporary solution. Sooner or later they will have to return home and deal with the issues that have made them angry. Talking about problems before they reach this point must be a better way of dealing with them. It is much better for both partners to settle any arguments before one of them decides to go out for a while to escape the situation. It may be that they will then decide to spend their time together instead.

I believe that men will have to become increasingly vigilant if they want to save their relationships. Women today are finding their own many and varied solutions to stress. That is why the home should have a peaceful, loving atmosphere – not one where its occupants are continually looking for a means of escape.

It is surprising how little people know about each other, even though they are sharing the same space. Many are blind to the uniqueness of the personality who is sharing their lives, and that can be a huge problem. If one partner becomes more successful than the other, this ignorance of their qualities can accelerate into jealousy which can be dangerous if it is not curbed from the beginning. Men especially have difficulty coping with a wife who is a success in her own right – for so long they have been the head of the household, but now women want to have their say in domestic and financial matters. However, it takes a long time to convince the older generations that they need to change their attitude in this regard. But change they must if they want their marriages to last.

There are some men who will keep their furniture well past its sell-by date rather than spend money replacing it. I have had women weeping in my healing room as they describe their shabby homes. It is not as if these men were financially embarrassed in any way – quite the reverse. In fact, this apparently small problem may seem irrelevant to those who are struggling to put meals on the table, but everyone has their limit, and irritating habits can lead to disaster if they are not dealt with quickly.

Long ago, most of the population lived happily at their own levels. Working class people who were able to rise above the poverty line were regarded as a success by their families and friends. These days, young people all start out with good intentions, but life is still a struggle. Now everyone is looking to become an instant millionaire, as though this will solve all their problems. It might solve some, but this kind of success comes with a huge price tag of its own – health and happiness. I have had to heal people like this. So many disregard the harm they are doing to their mind and body until it is too late. They believe their health is less important than having the chance to settle their debts. Take my advice – never underestimate the negative aspects of becoming rich or famous.

It seems that men especially go overboard – buying expensive cars and large houses. No matter how nice they were before the event, they cannot fight the need for a playboy image once they have the necessary cash to show off.

I have had to give counselling to whole families

who have all expressed a desire to be normal again once they have experienced the other side of the coin. The women especially wanted to return to a more normal way of life – above all, they missed the friends they had lost along the way.

Eventually, the men became bored with a lifestyle that was not only easy but in which they had no part to play; because they no longer had a need to succeed, they felt obsolete.

If you should become rich, through whatever means, keep a cool head, stay where you are for at least a year, and think your life through. That way you may avoid the pitfalls that others have made.

Real wealth is in the power of the mind, which inspires and creates avenues that in turn will help others.

I, *a stranger and afraid*
In a world I never made.

Last Poems
A. E. Housman 1859–1936

CHAPTER 14

Children and Teenagers

Thousands of children have poured out their hearts to me whilst I was giving them healing. Many of them had visited me because they could no longer cope with the strained relationships at home. Some of the stories I heard were heartbreaking, but most were just plain sad. One of the major emotions that came out was the feeling of fear the children experienced whenever they heard their parents arguing. They told me that they never knew whether the argument was going to turn violent or whether it would just peter out, and it was whilst waiting for this outcome that their fears would turn to terror. I believe it is essential for parents to think about this when they are having a disagreement – a parent who will cut the argument short is a parent who cares.

A child's mental health can be severely damaged by his or her inability to understand what is going on and how it is going to end. Any heated discussion lasting more than a few minutes will damage the psyche of a young child. Children only have a level of intelligence that befits their age. And while many parents may feel that their child is of above average intelligence, they must take into account that this does not extend to those tricky areas involving the emotions. Most children are completely baffled by the disagreements that lead to aggression and family upheavals.

Most adults are not aware that a bad atmosphere in the house can be charged with negative energy, which can affect every member of the household. The younger the child, the more susceptible they are to these worrying vibrations. Sometimes their minds can be so badly affected that it triggers illnesses, and many asthma attacks are caused by living in a negative environment.

When these children are taken to see their doctor, they may become even more agitated, knowing that they will be expected to give an account of how this attack started. Because they feel that they owe allegiance to their parents, they refuse to speak, and this can make the situation worse by accelerating the asthmatic condition. I know that there are many things that can trigger an asthmatic attack, but the emotional factor should never be ignored.

The peaceful atmosphere of my healing room, however, encouraged these children to open up, and when they did they talked their hearts out. There were tears too, but this is also part of the healing process; it has been scientifically proven that when we cry we rid ourselves of dangerous toxins.

Sometimes parents were surprised by some of the fears expressed by their child, but they were genuinely delighted that these problems had been aired. Up to that point they had been unable to get any information about how the attacks had started. Caring parents would always find this difficult to handle, as they would be well aware that something was troubling the child.

Withdrawal symptoms are also a sign that a child might be suffering emotional strain. Behaviour like this must never be ignored; no matter what the problem is, it will only get worse if it cannot be discussed and a solution found.

Although children grow up fast in today's society, young minds still have to be nurtured so that they can understand, at each stage in their lives, what they are supposed to do. Many adults believe that if a child is good at one thing they should show the same degree of talent for everything else. This causes an imbalance in the child's mind and body; eager to please, they will miss those very special years when they should behave like a child. I have heard many parents chide their very young children for being childish. They *are* children, and they should be able to behave in a childish manner. These years will never come again.

Even as an adult, you should always try to retain the 'child within'. It is the safety valve I know when things get bad. I have seen people laugh even though their lives have fallen to pieces, but no matter how crazy it may seem, humour is a safety valve, and it comes from the very centre of our being.

There are many children who suffer agonies because they know they will not be able to live up to their parents' expectations. Such fear also lowers their immune system, which means that these children are often ill. Children should be allowed to develop non-academic activities, something they enjoy alongside their ordinary studies. To drown a child in a sea of expectation is courting trouble. Try a little shared 'living' instead. You may be surprised at the result. Nearly all self-made millionaires have made it because they trusted their intuition and took chances. I have known many of them, and they could not be accused of being academic in any way!

Many children and teenagers take on the responsibility of covering up their family problems for fear of ridicule. Most like to boast that they have a happy home, because that is what they wish for themselves. Yet angry parents often turn on their children and blame them for discord in the family. 'Mummy said that if I hadn't been born, she could have left home.' I have heard this sentence a thousand times, and it is always shocking. The terrible mental damage inflicted on the child who hears this from a parent lasts a lifetime. This has been proved to me when I saw these children grow into adults; they told me that although they had forgiven, they couldn't forget, and that it was only the healing they received from time to time that had eased their path to maturity.

Many parents have spoken words like these in anger and then wonder why their child becomes introverted. But there can be no mitigating circumstances. An unhappy marriage can lead to a mental breakdown, and in this state logical thought disappears. Anger replaces logic, and compassion takes a back seat until things improve. In the meantime, children suffer – in an adult world they are the innocent targets.

If there are teenagers around prepared to answer back one angry word leads to another, eventually creating an atmosphere of hostility within the home that undermines the whole. Unfortunately the hurt inflicted on teenagers can be very damaging, so no matter how angry the parents might become, they have to realise that they are dealing with someone who is only just beginning to find out that they have to be responsible for their actions. Although most teenagers would not admit to being afraid at this stage, most of them are and this is why they have such negative reactions to small problems. If the parents could only encourage them to talk, they would be able to help them make sense of the world around them.

In short, small children and teenagers alike need someone to listen to them, and that ought to be their parents.

Some of the most appalling cases I have been asked to heal were children who had been physically or mentally abused. In these cases my mediumistic gifts proved to be a bonus because I was given detailed pictures of the assaults. Although I told their parents what I had seen, I did not discuss it with the patient, for during my years as a healer I have found the process of re-living a traumatic experience to be extremely damaging to the individual.

The best way to forget unpleasant incidents is to raise the level of consciousness, and this is done through healing. The patient will feel as though they are floating, and the unpleasant memories will begin to fade away. The reason for this is that the mind – not the brain – is the memory bank, and when the mind energy is raised it releases the temporary files from the brain.

I have studied the mind/brain phenomenon for thirty years and have seen this interaction through my clairvoyant abilities (as detailed in my book, *The Infinite Mind*). I have also seen the end results of the healing process in these cases, as have the parents, which is what really matters. The terrible truth was that in 60 per cent of the cases the abuse had been carried out by members of the children's own families. If these dreadful experiences are not erased quickly, they may carry them for the rest of their lives.

The perpetrators of these crimes are sick, and each and every one of them should have to spend time in a remedial hospital until they are well enough to be allowed out. This would not be as expensive as the treatment and possible hospitalisation of the victims, which in some cases can take months of care before they can leave a safe environment.

Many of these crimes would never have happened if the family and neighbours had been vigilant. I cannot recall how many times (but there were many) that people told me they could hear children screaming in adjacent houses but didn't want to interfere for fear of reprisals. If the children were simply being naughty, parents have nothing to fear and, assuming they are caring people, would be only too pleased that someone else was looking out for their children. If this was not so, then suspicion would be entirely justified.

Drugs and alcohol are steadily denuding the mental health of young people around the world. When they are in this drug-induced state, children are easy targets.

All parents should be vigilant. It puts a little more pressure on them, but nowhere near the pressure they will experience if their children are abused. Acting after the event, the courts can take years to sort out the mess. Vigilance, by every adult, could reduce the casualties.

Life used to be simple, but now it's getting more complicated by the day. In this technological age, young people are expected to become conversant with computers almost as soon as they can read. But this form of recreation is habit-forming, and the hours a child spends sitting in front of a screen should be monitored by adults. Television can also isolate family members from each other, because as they choose and watch programmes on their own, all conversation ceases.

Even TV adverts can be damaging, especially those which target children. Parents are constantly put under pressure to buy a new toy or gadget so that their children are seen to be 'with it' by their peers. Children often believe that it is their right to have these things, and if they don't get them, beware! We are bombarded with advertising, but an adult should have the sense to turn it off or turn away. Children need to be taught that they cannot automatically have everything they see, no matter how difficult this might make them!

Some of the children I counselled had become addicted to all the latest crazes and gadgets to the extent that it had become an illness with them.

Reversing this state of mind was as difficult as helping a drug addict to reform. Similarly, I was involved in healing both mind and body in teenagers who had spent so many years sitting in front of computer and television screens that they had developed physical and personality disorders. Instead of taking regular exercise some had completely isolated themselves from family and friends, preferring to talk to faceless people on the world-wide web. They had become sad, sad people who had lost the art of communicating on a one-to-one basis with a real person. Gradually re-introducing them to the real world was a painstaking task.

It is not easy being a parent, and there are always those who constantly blame the parents whose children misbehave. But even in happy households, it is common for one parent to say that a child is exactly like his or her partner when the youngster has misbehaved. What parents need to understand is that their child is a mixture of both sets of genes! Whether these remarks are made in jest or in anger, they have a negative effect on the children, who will grow up thinking that they've inherited only the worst side of *both* parents.

The world is changing fast, and there is nothing we can do about it. That is why it is even more important for children to be brought up in a loving home. One of the most valuable lessons they can learn is to give rather than receive. Try to help your children see the funny side of things. Children are excellent mimics, and they learn most of their craft from the people they live with.

When mothers came to me for healing, they invariably had to bring their young children with them, and the children would often join in the conversations we were having. They would talk about something that had happened, and their mothers would be taken aback by the child's view of events. One little girl mentioned that she was hungry. 'Mummy forgot to give me my breakfast,' she complained. The horrified woman asked the child why she hadn't reminded her. 'I tried to,' she said, 'but you told me to be quiet.' Of course her mother was mortified by the accusation, but it is something that can happen in every household at some time. This story gives you an insight into what is important in a child's mind. As with adults, food is linked with comfort and love, so the child wasn't just hungry – she felt neglected too.

I have asked teenagers whether they had become upset when their parents hadn't listened to them, and their replies were often surprising. They told me that they weren't particularly fazed when they were ignored, but it made them worry that if they were in real trouble their voice might not be heard. I think they have a valid point, as I have received dozens of survival messages from young people whose lives were lost in the home. In these cases, their parents were inevitably left with a sense of guilt that never deserted them. But they needed to be reassured that they are only human, and humans have many failings. Perfection would not last long in this world! And children can be so demanding that it is sometimes impossible to give them the attention they seek.

There are important issues in this chapter that need to be addressed and which could make life easier for everyone. Some of the saddest stories I have heard are from children of all ages who have been caught in the web of misery that threatens all when parents divorce.

There were tales of parents who tried to buy their children's loyalty with money and gifts. This is a particularly tricky situation, especially if one parent is financially more secure than the other. These parents demean the intelligence of their offspring if they believe that these ruses work. They don't. The children will still feel unhappy and unloved as they watch the disintegration of what was once a family unit. And even as their world is turned upside down, they are expected to support the parent they live with. It is a hard task for any child to cope with, though some of them do manage to make the most of a bad situation.

It was only when I gave these children healing that they let their defences down. When I had listened to their stories, I encouraged them to take a more positive view of life as far as their own future was concerned. I also reminded them that their parents were ordinary human beings who were no different from the rest of society. They made mistakes, and some of the choices they had made in their twenties might not continue to work as they mature.

Blame is an easy weapon when families are at war. However, it is better to learn to listen to everyone involved. There is no substitute for giving respect to each individual and trying to work out a compromise – this can move mountains!

Another very serious problem that can infect every member of the family is lying. Little white lies to protect someone can be OK if they are not used too often, but children soon pick up the art of lying and this can become a lifetime's habit – and one that will be extremely hard to kick.

I found that nearly all the children I came into contact with were very concerned when someone in their family had lied to them. The pain they felt was much worse if the lie had come from a parent – they had felt betrayed by the person they trusted most. 'How could they lie to me like that?' was a plea I was to hear time and time again. Although the lie may not have seemed important to the adults, it had sunk deep into the children's soul. They simply could not forget. Worse, they felt they could never believe another word that person said.

All children like to think that their parents are

squeaky clean and could not possibly say or do anything wrong. But unfortunately life isn't like that. There are times, however, when it is not appropriate to tell the truth. Rather than lie, there are ways and means of covering up that wouldn't have such a catastrophic effect on the children if the truth were found out.

Habitual liars are always found out. They may then become isolated from family and friends, and their lives will be lonely and miserable.

One of the most significant lies I have come across in my years of healing is that used by some adoptive parents when they make the decision not to tell their child that he or she has been adopted. There are often mitigating circumstances, and sometimes it is not always possible to tell the truth. But these children do have a very real problem when they find that they are not living with their birth parents. Some parents who did not tell the truth admitted that they had made the biggest mistake of their lives. One lie had led to another, and this had left them with a permanent feeling of guilt. The manifestation of guilt is ill health. Telling the truth whenever possible is the best way to ensure that your child will have the best possible start in life.

It is important to remember that young children can be extremely psychic – and they will instinctively know when something doesn't add up. They become more and more inquisitive, and they take great pride in the fact that they have a complete family unit, especially when grandparents are involved. Most of the children I saw were very proud of their extended family groups and were always telling me about them, especially if a particular relative had a special talent.

A sense of belonging is very important to children, and that is why they suffer so much if they accidentally find out that they have been adopted. Some children I saw reacted by going into a deep depression, and over the years I have had to pick up the pieces and try to heal their wounds. The most common remark I heard them make was that they had felt like complete fool, especially if they had told their friends of a talent they thought they had inherited from their adoptive family.

Another phrase I often heard was, 'When I look back at my life, I realise that it's all been a farce.' The realisation that they were living with people with whom they had no blood ties had destroyed them. On the other hand, children who are told from the start that they are adopted are usually quite relaxed about it. They had been made to feel special because they had been chosen.

Trying to decide on the right thing to do can be extremely difficult. What these children have said to me over the years is important. If I help their cause by giving them a voice, then my time has not been wasted.

PART THREE

Freeing the Spirit

I am not yet born; O fill me
With strength against those who would freeze my
humanity, would dragoon me into a lethal automaton,
would make me a cog in a machine, a thing with
one face, a thing, and against all those
who would dissipate my entirety, would
blow me like thistledown hither and
thither or hither and thither
like water held in the
hands would spill me.
let them not make me a stone and let them not spill me
Otherwise kill me.

Prayer Before Birth
Louis MacNeice 1907–1963

CHAPTER 15

Charisma

Charisma is a God-given gift. People with charisma have an exceptional ability to attract and influence others. It is a magnetism that can either enslave or free those who encounter it. However, if it is used to enslave others, then the person with the charismatic personality will eventually lose their power. Conversely, if used for the benefit of others and for healing, this power can become so formidable that it can take the one who is so endowed to such great heights that they could change the world. These people are very rare.

I have met both types – the good and the bad – and it is the latter who initially made the greatest impact. Most of these have been people at the top of every profession you can name.

But it is when you meet the grey people in between – those who have found fame by working the good and bad sides of their charisma into a complex tapestry – that you have to take notice of your gut feeling. You have to know when to bow out.

People who are spiritually inclined are often naturally reclusive and have an aura of serenity that is easy to recognise. The secret of their success is their ability to steal as many quiet moments as their career allows. For them, calmness of mind and clarity of thought are essential, especially if they are expected to make life-saving decisions. These people do not have to boast or shout. Their abilities are immediately obvious to those around them, and that is why the most successful are quiet in word and action.

This does not mean that their lives will sail along on an easy course. Quite the reverse. For although charisma is a priceless gift, it does not come free. Therefore, payback time is never ending. At the end of one rocky path there will be another. But on these paths these people learn to accept the unacceptable, and when they do this, fear of the unknown is cast out for ever.

Some people believe that the spiritually charismatic will also be endowed with a physical beauty. Very few have both, in fact, but if you look into their eyes, you will have a soul-to-soul experience that could change your life. Those who have experienced this have likened it to being struck by lightning!

Like many things, the invisible is far greater and more interesting than the visible, so many of the most wonderful thoughts and visions are left to the few who seek inspiration from a higher source. It is from this source that those who have not been born with a natural charisma can gain an insight into the secrets of this type of personality and claim a charm of their own. Although it may not be magnetic in substance, it could still have a dramatic influence on their lives and those around them.

It is important to seek the meaning of life, to look outside your own particular environment and to find solace from the wisdom of ages, where sages of the past have exposed their weaknesses so that others may learn from them. This is the main reason why you will find so many quotations in my books – to learn from the wisdom of the past.

If you wish to add a touch of charm to your personality, then you must seek spiritual knowledge. This kind of knowledge does not come gift-wrapped, you have to work at it. There is no 'gain without pain'.

Young people believe that if they overcome the pain threshold in one area, it is a lifetime's payment. Unfortunately this is not true. What it does teach us, however, is how we, as individuals, can deal with it. Those who learn from this pain are those who will eventually gain that little bit of extra charm.

If you wish to extend the lessons and reach for the stars, then you must seek knowledge. For knowledge is a mighty weapon when combating ignorance, and there will be plenty of that around to challenge what you have gained. But knowledge alone will not give you the edge. You must also have a decent vocabulary if you wish to go to greater heights.

Discipline must be your constant companion, for when you feel less disposed than usual to turn the pages in the book of learning, a little discipline will see to it that you keep your part of the bargain which you entered into when you chose this path.

If you have the strength to put yourself through these stages, you will not be disappointed. For you will be endowed as if by magic with that little bit of charm and charisma that will get you through.

Footfalls echo in the memory
Down the passage which we did not take
Towards the door we never opened
Into the rose-garden. My words echo
Thus, in your mind . . .
human kind
Cannot bear very much reality.

'Burnt Norton', *Four Quartets*
T. S. Eliot 1888–1965

CHAPTER 16

Signposts

Throughout our lives, we will be given signposts. If we do not recognise them, or simply wish to ignore them, then our journey will be long and hard.

From birth, we are guided by a spiritual guardian, who will place the signs along the way when they are needed. If you have faith, then you will see them.

Sometimes, the reason for a particular sign will be immediately apparent. It could well be a warning or a lifeline that you will need in the future.

Knowing that there are signposts in our lives will make it easier for us to recognise them when they appear. It will be your choice whether or not to react to them. However, if you decide to take the easy way out and simply accept or dismiss these signs as the mood takes you, you might well miss the most important sign of all. From that point it will be downhill all the way unless you have the courage to walk the rocky path to get back on course again.

From a young age, I always had the ability to read

these signposts, although I have only been able to analyse them in retrospect. To help you to read your own signposts more accurately, I am going to give you an account of the signs that have helped me.

Before the last war I lived in Kennington, London, and although I lived in a nice area, there were streets nearby that were off-limits. They were dark, dank and narrow – so narrow, in fact, that even the sun's rays were blotted out from the pavements.

My friends and I used to run past these streets as though the devil was after us. Someone told me that the people who lived in those houses would take the clothes off your back, and – as children do – I took this literally.

One day, I accidentally found myself at the entrance to one these streets. I was about to turn around when I found that my path was blocked by a group of shabby children who were calling me names. I had no idea how I had got there, but I was always a dreamer so it would have been easy for me to take a wrong turning. Women standing on their doorsteps stared at me, but made no attempt to help me. I tried to run, but my feet were rooted to the ground with fear. Then a young woman walked towards me and asked me where I lived. I told her, and she said, 'If you wait here, I'll get a shawl and walk you to the end of the road.' On the way out of the street, she asked me if my mother loved me, and

I told her that she did. She smiled. 'You know, the people in this street are no different from where you live. We love our children too.' Before she said goodbye, she smiled again and said, 'You have a lot to learn, kid. The next time you pass by, come and see me. If anyone worries you, tell them you're going to see Jess, then they won't touch you.'

It was a long time before I had the courage to knock on her door, but one day I felt as though someone was pushing me towards her house. It was a weird feeling, as if I had no control over my actions. When Jess opened the door to me, she was all smiles. 'Well, if it isn't the kid,' she said. Although the house was tiny, I could see that it was clean and tidy. The kitchen table was in the middle of the room, and she sat me down and gave me some milk.

Two boys rushed in and shouted, 'What's she doing here?' Jess told them to 'Get out and leave us alone.' Once they'd gone, she asked me where I lived, and about my parents. When I'd finished speaking, she said, 'I knew you were posh. It's written all over you.' She leaned forward. 'Now I'll tell you about my life.'

I visited Jess for two years, and although I was only eight years old when we first met, she talked to me as if I were an adult. She told me what poverty meant to her and what it did to the people who suffered from it. 'You can't give in, kid,' she said. 'You just have to get on with it and hope that

211

something better is around the corner. Hope, that's what keeps us all going. You'll probably never know what hunger is and what it does to you.' She sighed. 'It's the children I worry about.'

Eventually, the children in that street accepted me as Jess's little friend, and they never threatened me again.

One day, wondering where on earth I vanished to after school, my mother followed me, and I introduced her to Jess. They became friends, and my mother was able to help many people in the street through her work with the church, even though most of them vowed they would never set foot in a church themselves. 'God never helped us, so why should we sing His praises?' they'd say. Fortunately my mother had a great sense of humour, and as we were walking home she said with a smile, 'I can see their point.'

For me, this experience was the beginning of understanding, and I have never forgotten Jess and the valuable lessons I learnt sitting at her kitchen table. People are not poor because they want to be. It is the hand that fate has dealt them. But even in the most dire of circumstances, there was laughter, love and hope.

In those days, Kennington was a mixture of the well-heeled and the poverty-stricken. It was this combination that inspired the have-nots to aspire to great heights, and many of them succeeded. I have never since lived in a community where there was such a plethora of talent put to good use.

Charlie Chaplin, the great actor and film director, was born in Kennington in 1889. The poignant contrasts of humour and sadness in his films mirrored his early life.

Lillian Baylis, the English theatrical agent who managed the Old Vic theatre and who became famous for her ability to have both Shakespeare and opera under the same roof, was often seen in the pews of our church. At mass one Sunday, this great lady approached my aunt and said, 'This child should have singing lessons. She has a great voice.' Turning to the people gathered around us, she said, 'If you have talent, don't waste it. I believe this child will make her mark in life.' Then, leaning heavily on her walking stick, she turned and walked away. It was the last time we saw her. She died in 1937.

My aunt was thrilled to bits but for all the wrong reasons. She was simply overcome by the fact that Lillian Baylis had noticed us at all, as she was a formidable lady and rarely spoke to anyone. But there is no doubt in my mind that she felt compelled to speak to us, to plant the seed that was to grow later in life. My guide was on course.

There is no way that Jess could have guessed how much her words helped me when I was evacuated at the beginning of the war. I was taken to a house where there was no love, laughter, or hope – and even worse (for me at least) no food. Like all children I had always lived for my food, and I shall remember the hunger pangs I experienced for those three years I spent in that house for the rest of my life.

Because the woman of the house to where I was evacuated was such an ogre, I was too frightened to write to my mother and tell her the truth. All I could do was hope that someone would save me. I eventually found the courage to move myself to a better home, though without the housing officer's approval.

The courage that Jess had shown in dire circumstances had left an imprint on my mind that helped me to survive. Once I had made the effort to face up to life and the negative people that surrounded me at that time, I was able to live my life the way I wanted to.

Although there were many beautiful trees in Kennington, they were in places like roadsides and parks, which made it difficult to climb them without being noticed. In any event, I had never had the slightest inclination to climb them. But now I was living in the country, surrounded by fields and trees, and there I found *my* cedar tree. Another signpost had been placed on my path, because one night I was drawn to this tree like a magnet. It was dark, and I had been locked out of my home while my foster parents enjoyed an evening at the local cinema. They would not allow me to stay in the house by myself but told me to sit in the porch until their return.

Alone and frightened, I walked to the end of the road, and there it was, standing at the edge of a small green. My cedar tree. I had seen it before in daylight, but in the dark it beckoned to me. Heaving myself from branch to branch, I made my way to the top of the tree – and that was the first time I had ever really seen the night sky. I saw a thousand stars looking down at me, and I thought I had gone to heaven. I felt that my home was 'out there', and I wanted to return to it. That was the beginning of my life-long interest in meditation. Somehow, I knew that if I looked long enough, I would be transported to another world. Which of course I was.

One sign led to another, and within months I could see spirits walking through my bedroom at night. I was frightened and would hide under the bedclothes.

Now I believe those spirits were there to protect me. One night, a bomb dropped into the field outside the house. All the windows were shattered by the blast, and in the morning a large sliver of glass was found embedded in the headboard of my bed. If I hadn't disappeared under the bedclothes when the spirits were present, it would have pierced my face or head. Once I had recovered from this trauma, the spirits disappeared.

*   *   *

I returned home before the war ended. My mother had found us a house in Surrey after a bomb had reduced our London home to rubble. We still had to take cover whenever there was an air-raid, but at least I was back in the family fold.

When my mother asked me what I intended to do when I left school, I told her that I wanted to be a vet. I remember the look of horror on her face, as she was not at all enamoured of animals in any way. Even though I was offered a job as a trainee vet, she refused to let me take it. I was heartbroken. My signpost had been pulled out of the ground and dashed aside by someone else. Or so I thought. But in retrospect, I can now see that I was being shown that we cannot construct our own signs, especially those of ambition. We must always remember that these signposts are of a spiritual nature and are put there so that we may learn as we go along.

Although the bombs were still dropping towards the end of the war, I accepted a job in London, delivering advertising plates to Fleet Street newspapers in return for a secretarial course. There were several signposts here, and I spent far more hours than I should have loitering and listening to the people who made the news. I never wanted to become a journalist, but as I listened to them talking about their work, I became hooked on knowledge and on the wonder of words.

My mother loved her weekly magazine, particularly the love stories, so my first attempt at writing was a short love story. I thought that if my mother liked it, I would follow this path to find out how much potential I had and to see whether I could make a career out of writing. She loved the first story and couldn't wait for the next. Unfortunately, she had to wait for ever, for although I began many stories, I never finished another.

I had not yet learned the most important lesson in life, which was that nothing would ever be finished without discipline. This is especially true if you want to be a writer, because it is a lonely and solitary life. Through this exercise, I learned for myself that fiction was not for me. Even to this day I cannot read fiction.

When I read a non-fiction book, I have to feel all the emotions that run through it. I have to laugh and cry with the author, to feel their joy and their pain. It is only through other people's experiences that we learn we are not the only person on the planet who has sunk to the depths and – like the phoenix – has had to find the strength to rise from those ashes and start again.

There is an added bonus from this kind of experience, which is that we are not only wiser but more resilient than we were before – and that gives us power.

*   *   *

My next signpost came in the form of a young Canadian soldier who visited our home after my mother met him at a local concert. She had taken pity on him because he had looked so lost and forlorn. He asked my mother if he could take me to a dance, and we became close friends.

One day, when I asked him about his family, he blushed and said that he didn't want to talk about them. I thought this was strange, and continued to question him until eventually he said, 'I come from a North American tribe, who live on a reservation.' I looked at him.

'So what?' I asked.

He was quiet for a while, and then he said, 'I will understand it if you don't want to see me again.' I was very young, and had no idea why he should think in this way. Then he explained that although his government wanted him to fight for them, they had never done anything for his family. He was very bitter about the way his people had been treated.

All I knew about these tribes came from films about the Red Indians, and I couldn't quite come to terms with the fact that I was actually looking at one in a Canadian military uniform. But listening to his history and to the incredible stories of his ancestors, I became hooked. I wanted to stay with him all my life and live in a wigwam. Fortunately for me, my mother soon squashed this idea.

I last saw him when I waved goodbye as he boarded

a train for London, which was to take him on the first leg of his journey to the Italian front. Although he promised to write every day, I only received three letters, and I thought he had forgotten me.

Later that year his friend called on me to tell me that he had died within a month of landing in Italy and that they had shared his last moments. The friend handed me the letters I'd sent, and said, 'These were in his pocket. He carried them everywhere he went; they meant so much to him.'

Because I was so young, his death had a great impact on me, and to this day I can remember the grief and despair that came with the knowledge that I would never see him again.

Years later, I remembered the stories about the spirits of his ancestors and how they still looked after their tribes. And I remembered his words: 'Death is the beginning, not the end.' We had been destined to meet, and our friendship taught me a lot.

It is strange that many people have told me that a North American Indian with long dark hair and aquiline features often overshadows me when I heal. I like to think that maybe one of my Canadian friend's ancestors is looking after me. As I have never mentioned this episode to anyone but a few close friends, especially as I have deliberately discouraged any fantasies about spirit guides, there is no way that my patients could possibly have known of my history.

This young man touched my life in a way that

he would never know. His legacies to me were the memories that have never faded, and my life-long interest in the plight of the American tribes and the humiliation that has been heaped upon their people.

It was at about the same time that a neighbour of ours, who was a teacher, offered to pay for my musical education. My mother refused the offer, but it raised my hopes that one day I would become a professional opera singer, and I spent all my spare time studying opera and mimicking the great opera stars of that era. There is no doubt that someone was encouraging me to 'follow my star'. And later, I had the opportunity to do just that.

It was only when I became a singer that I grew fascinated by the hands of the other performers. As they used their hands to express themselves, I noticed that each and every one of them had their own unique patterns in the palms of their hands, and I decided to study hand analysis. Backstage, in the intervals during rehearsals, was the ideal time to put my hobby into practice.

As the years progressed I graduated from ordinary hand analysis to medical and criminal studies. It was fascinating.

One case I particularly remember from these medical studies was that of a blind man who had been brilliant at reading braille. After his death, the skin on his fingertips was removed and it was found that he had actually grown a form of optic nerve in the tips of his fingers!

During this period I had a small medical problem that left me fatigued most of the time. My GP offered me tranquillisers, which at the time I thought was astonishing. I wanted to wake up, not go to sleep!

The sign I had at this point in my life was quite magical. I came across a small shop which had a few weird-looking packages in the window, and for some reason I decided to go inside and investigate its contents further. The shelves were full of herbal concoctions, together with bottles of vitamins and minerals, and dried roots that hung from the ceiling. You need to remember that at this point, over forty-six years ago, no one had ever heard of health shops. Of course I had heard of herbalists, but there were very few people who discussed this form of medicine. Many believed that it had something to do with witchcraft. Thankfully in this day and age we are more enlightened.

Before I left the shop, I made one small purchase, which was a little pocket book on natural remedies by Barbara Cartland. It was the best buy I have ever made. Inside was not only a case history that mirrored my own but also the natural remedy for it.

I rushed back to the shop, bought the remedy, and within a few days I was back to normal. From that day, I read every book and every white paper devoted to vitamin, mineral and cell therapy, and eventually became a therapist myself. Much later I was able to link this career with my emerging gift of healing.

The experience also set me on a path of learning that has no end. New discoveries are being made all the time, and the medical profession is now looking at expanding its own knowledge by considering folk remedies that have been used for centuries.

Indigenous peoples have always found remedies for their particular problems in the areas in which they live. We would be wise to look more deeply into this aspect of natural healing, for it makes a lot of sense.

I tried very hard to follow the private signposts in my life, but after the death of my mother, and while suffering from other heartaches, I decided to live abroad. My life in Spain and my subsequent return to this country have already been recorded in my previous books, as has the failure of the medical profession to identify another health problem that made me seek out a medium. I must admit, I was not inclined to take the advice I received very seriously, although I was impressed when the medium told me that I had been healing all my life. When I denied this, he said, 'But you have been reading hands, haven't you? You may have thought you were simply giving a hand reading, but because you are a natural healer, these people were also being given healing.'

*   *   *

In retrospect I knew he was right. I had indeed been giving vitamin and mineral analysis at these readings, but my friends had often seemed to recover even before they had time to buy the vitamins.

The medium also told me that I had been a very obstinate woman and had not heeded the messages that were being given to me. I thought he was talking about mediumistic messages, which of course I was not getting at that time, but now I realise that it is our signposts which are the messages, and for the layman they are easier to read and understand.

It is time for you to recall your own signposts, from the beginning of your life to the present day. You will recognise those you have misread and those you have understood, but the real value of this exercise is that it will give you an insight into your own character and spirituality – and an insight into why certain things happened to you when they did. The art of sign reading is invaluable. We all have our own unique blueprint. Keep faith with yourself and the signs will become easier to read.

Clairvoyance means 'clear sight'. As the clarity of the messages becomes stronger, so will this particular gift. But I must warn you not to attempt to read the signposts of others. It is their life, and they have to find their own meanings for themselves. How else will they learn?

We are the music makers,
We are the dreamers of dreams,
Wandering by lone sea-breakers,
And sitting by desolate streams;
World-losers and world-forsakers,
On whom the pale moon gleams:
We are the movers and shakers
Of the world for ever, it seems.

Ode
Arthur O'Shaughnessy 1844–1881

CHAPTER 17

Daydreams

Everyone daydreams – sinking into a relaxed state, perhaps dreaming of future success. Although many of these dreams will never materialise in the form in which we see them, the time spent daydreaming will not have been wasted. This practice activates the mind, which in turn expands and links up with a Universal energy that stimulates and leads us on to other paths. In the long term, those paths will probably match our talents and be more to our liking.

So what happens to our mind when we enter the world of daydreaming, where we can – with so little effort – shape the images that may change our lives?

By deliberately sinking into a state where dreams can materialise, we give our mind the freedom that is so necessary to its development. In this state it can access information from all sources, especially those in which we have a particular interest. Mind energy, like any other, attracts like to like, and the kind of information we seek will be picked up by like minds, which will then send thoughts and pictures to absorb in our trance-like state. Most people believe that these pictures and messages come from the imagination, and of course they do. But what is the imagination if it isn't the mind?

When we relax and start daydreaming, we immediately propel ourselves into dimensions that would otherwise be closed to us. And when we touch the Universal Mind, we enter a source of knowledge so great that it can overwhelm in its intensity. That is when we must cast our doubts aside and listen to the silence, for contained therein are the great truths. If we take the time to access it, this formidable library of knowledge is ours for the asking.

From the matter which we can see around us, we draw those things which enable us to survive. But if it was only these things that were responsible for our survival, then we would become lost souls, locked into a void from which there is no escape. However, if we give our minds the freedom they need to inspire us, then physical and mental health can be maintained in a way that allows us to continually move into new pastures on our way to our chosen destination.

Once the art of daydreaming has been acquired, it can never be lost, because it forges a path through negative energies into a light that enters the soul and inspires.

I have known thousands of people who, though physically crippled, have used daydreaming as a means to exercise their bodies. Under these circumstances, the interaction between the mind and the brain has stimulated nerves and muscles to such an extent that the person can actually feel the sensations of running, dancing or whatever else they would be inclined to do were they able. I have always recommended this form of exercise for those who have been physically damaged and I have received thousands of letters from all around the world giving me detailed descriptions of the physical and mental progress these people have achieved. Many of them had overcome their disabilities to such an extent that they had been able to reverse the damage and lead more normal lives.

Students have also found daydreaming a means by which they can access the Universal Mind and cut out stress. Many children are subjected to unacceptable levels of stress, from the time they start school until they graduate. Although educational authorities believe they are addressing the stress factor by introducing physical exercise, this is not enough. I have healed many students by introducing them to daydreaming, and where they had previously been overwhelmed by the educational system and its pressures, they were able to sail through their exams.

A few universities have added meditation classes

to their extra-curricular activities, and although this is commendable, some of the students find that it is too channelled and simply adds to their stress and their inability to relax. It takes time to learn how to meditate, but we are born with the ability to daydream, and if this gift is nurtured, meditation could be the next step.

You cannot ignore the spiritual side of the individual, and by that I do not mean religion. Spirituality is the end result of the kind of thinking that takes the unique mind out of this dimension and into a realm where dreams can become reality. The invisible realm is the powerhouse that lights the fire in the imagination and attracts inspirational thought. Set your mind free, and it will seek out information that has been previously withheld from you.

When I introduced the idea of daydreaming to students, their first reaction was sometimes one of complete amazement. Many argued that time was of the essence and that the time 'wasted' on this exercise would only exacerbate their problems. But I asked them to trust me, to put aside fifteen minutes a day for two weeks, and then give me the results.

At the end of this period, they all told me that not only had there been a marked improvement in their work, but that they had enjoyed the experience so much that it had easily become part of their daily routine. Over the years I watched their progress, and they all achieved their aims and went on to even greater heights.

Many people who have reached the top of their profession also use daydreaming as a means of achieving their goals. They would probably call it 'gut feeling' rather than inter-dimensional communication, but whatever the name, the end results are the same.

The Earth is a living organism, and like all organisms will retaliate when it feels that it is being abused. That is why there are so many floods, fires, storms, volcanic eruptions and natural disasters, which are getting worse as man inflicts more and more indignities on the planet. The same is true with the Mind. If it does not have the freedom it needs to accumulate information for the good of the mind, body and soul, it will rebel, and the ensuing storms will incapacitate the human body as well as the mind/brain connections.

But how do we know if we have achieved a connection with the Universal Mind while we're daydreaming? When we have finished relaxing in this way, we often feel as though we have not only lost track of time but are in a void where the process of thought has come to a halt. This is actually a good result. Information that we receive in this way does not manifest via the brain for twelve hours or more, but when it does it will come through as though it is your own original conscious thought.

If you wish to test this, daydream for a week or so, and keep a journal of your thoughts during this time. Then stop daydreaming for two weeks, write your thoughts down again, and compare the results. I think you will find the different levels of inspirational ideas that come to you impressive.

A close friend came to see me, and asked for my advice. She told me that she worked a ten-hour day and then spent her evenings trying to catch up with the usual household chores. It was obvious from her appearance that her health had deteriorated, and she admitted that she felt that she could no longer keep to this regime of 'all work and no play'. Like most of the population, she worked long hours because she needed the money, and that was her dilemma.

I suggested that she should put one hour aside every evening and daydream. 'But I could be "doing something" in that time,' she argued. I told her that she *would* be "doing something", as she would be freeing her mind from the prison she had built around it. She continued to argue until I asked her where she would like to travel if she had the necessary time and money. Closing her eyes, she gave me a detailed description of a small hilltop village in Italy which she had visited in her teens. 'I can see it now, and the perfume from the orange and lemon blossom was incredible.' Breathing deeply, she said, 'I can still smell it.'

Opening her eyes, she said, 'What an idiot I am.

No wonder I feel like this – I haven't taken a holiday for years.'

I asked her what she thought she was doing when she was visualising her Italian village. 'Day-dreaming?' she asked sheepishly.

I smiled. 'You will find it will give you all sorts of answers,' I told her.

So why didn't I suggest that she just take a holiday? Because it wouldn't have introduced her to something that she could use every day, from which she could initiate her own response. It is much better when the mind stretches out and returns with the answers, as the individual needs to feel that it was their idea. That is also a form of freedom.

Nurturing a natural gift can help you to achieve the impossible dream.

Weary with toil, I haste me to my bed,
The dear repose for limbs with travel tired;
But then begins a journey in my head
To work my mind, when body's work's expired.

Sonnets, 27
William Shakespeare 1564–1616

CHAPTER 18

Mind Journeys

As in the sonnet opposite, the mind journeys that I have taken while asleep cannot be counted because of their spasmodic nature – and because I've forgotten most of them! Fortunately, I have remembered those which came when I needed them most. In many I was given a clear vision of the future, and this knowledge gave me the strength and courage to follow through, even though the ideas often led me into difficult arenas where I was constantly challenged.

In this chapter, I will take you to places that you may never see but which are in the cosmos somewhere (or else I wouldn't have seen them!). They are not dreams, because I have learnt to recognise the difference between a dream and a mind journey – their differing images are instantly recognisable.

I have given this chapter a lot of thought. I have always felt privileged to have been able to embark upon these journeys, and at one time I thought that sharing them with others would weaken the energy of the images, thoughts and actions. But now I also believe that they are experiences that should be shared for the good of all. There is a message for everyone in these tales, and I hope that you will find answers here that may have eluded you in the past.

I was walking across a desert towards the setting sun, which glowed and shimmered on the horizon. As I looked at it, the orange and red hues sent up images of fiery fingers of flame which seemed to be grasping at the force fields surrounding them, giving the impression that the sun didn't want to leave.

As I walked towards the sunset I could feel the hot sand burning the soles of my feet. I knew that I could not rest, and that I had to go on until I reached my destination.

Then everything changed. I was sitting by a waterfall, and someone was holding a cup to my lips. As I sipped the clear water, a disembodied voice said, 'Rest a while. This is not the end of the journey, but the beginning.'

This was my first mind journey, and although it was given to me a long time ago, the memory still remains. At the time the meaning didn't register, and I was only to learn its significance as I continued to live my life. The fiery fingers were the danger zones I encountered whilst walking a spiritual path, and the clear water was the essence that would sustain me through the heat.

There was chaos everywhere and I was trying to fly through it, but as I did so I had to go through zones of misery and despair. I avoided the worst areas by picking up speed until I reached the perimeters.

Then the scene changed, and I found myself sitting in an empty room. I relished the silence after my stormy journey.

Someone entered the room and sat beside me. 'You were lucky to get here in one piece. Why didn't you ask for help?'

At this time I was trying to make sense of my new career as a medium and healer – a career that had never remotely entered into my dreams of the future. But after this particular journey I paid heed, and from that point on I always asked for help when new experiences threatened to overwhelm me. The way that help has been given has never ceased to amaze me.

I was walking through a valley when the scenery changed and I found myself in a totally different landscape. Surrounded by forest and rocks, I could see no means of escape. Looking back, I found that the path had disappeared and was now thick with trees which rose sharply to the top of a mountain.

Panicking, I ran back and forth, trying without success to find an easy route through this difficult terrain. I tried to clamber up one of the hills until I was prevented from going any further by dense, thorny bushes.

Turning back, I found that the hills had changed into stony mountain paths. I was so exhausted I sat down on the hard ground and wondered how I was going to escape from this prison-like environment.

Then I had an inspirational thought. If the mind was so powerful, I could re-shape the landscape to suit my needs. I then began a series of mind exercises, mentally turning the hills into flat land, reducing the mountains to small hillocks, and carving a path through the landscape so that I could return home.

When I awoke, I knew without any doubt that I had been given a priceless thought: no matter what obstacles I might encounter throughout my life, I could reduce their capacity to harm through visualisation and through the fact that mind power can move mountains. Whatever problems we are faced with in this life, we can minimise the danger – especially to our health – by refusing to allow them to become a permanent fixture in our psyche.

I was sitting amid a circle of people. Some wore white robes, while others were dressed in their normal clothes.

There was a discussion in progress, but I couldn't hear the words. Then I understood that they were communicating telepathically. Heated words were being exchanged by two men in normal attire, and the temperature was such that I felt as though I was sitting in a Turkish bath.

Then one of the figures in white asked the men to stand up and share their grievances. The first man spoke for a long time. Eventually the second man stood up – and then, without uttering a single word, sat down again.

The man in the white robe said, 'You have both proved a point.' Looking at the man who had talked and talked, he said, 'You need to learn to listen, and you can't do that until you stop speaking.' Turning to the other, he said, 'And when you are given the opportunity to make an impact, we find that you have nothing to say. But you have both taught us all an invaluable lesson through your egos – and that is that the person who talks all the time learns nothing, and the one who says nothing has such contempt for the rest of us that he refuses to enlighten us in any way.'

It needs courage to spill out our thoughts, but we all have a 'need to know'.

The sky was blue, and the sea was so calm that it shimmered gently in the sunlight. The horizon seemed to be bathed in a silver light, which was so unusual that I decided to investigate. I walked into the water and began to swim. There was no doubt in my mind that I would reach my destination.

I was a long way from shore when storm clouds began to gather, changing the colour of the sea from blue to dark grey in a matter of minutes. I wanted to turn back, but something was urging me to finish the task I had set myself. Huge waves washed over me, and as the sea turned into a cauldron, I could feel myself being sucked under. But my survival instinct took hold and I fought back. For some reason I never felt that I would drown.

When I finally reached the silvery light, I bathed myself in its glow, and felt uplifted and blessed.

My first reaction when I opened my eyes was one of elation. Later, when I had time to analyse it, I realised that the mind journey depicted the upheaval I was going through at that time. The storm that was happening in my personal life was threatening to drown me, and yet I knew intuitively that I would win through. At no time during this episode did I ever feel like giving up. There was too much at stake – chiefly my spiritual survival. The knowledge that (with tremendous effort) I would eventually stand in the light inspired me to bury the past and go on to new pastures.

This particular mind journey told me what I already knew, but the fact that it had clearly shown me a future where I would eventually reach the light gave me the courage to fulfil all the promises I had made to myself.

I was standing in the middle of a department store when someone came up to me and told me I could have whatever I desired and that they would take care of the bill.

There was so much to choose from that my previously peaceful state of mind became chaotic. What should I choose? How would I get everything home? Where would I put it all once I got there? I had so little time to spare in my life that I knew the contents of the parcels would probably never see the light of day. These questions were never ending.

I made the decision to turn away from temptation so that my thoughts could be directed to calmer waters and to peace of mind. I was also given the thought that you should be suspicious of 'strangers who come bearing gifts'.

This experience taught me that worldly goods are of no worth if you have to go through a period of confusion to get them. There is no substitute for peace of mind. It also taught me that we do not need 90 per cent of the things we strive so hard to own.

The warning about strangers bearing gifts has come true all too often through the years. Ignoring it has caused havoc in many people's lives – including my own. True friends will seek you out, even if you live in a hut. The others are best left alone.

Relaxing in an armchair, I looked out of the window and saw that it was raining. Putting on my coat, I walked out of the house and started to run down the road, desperately trying to hold an umbrella over my head. As the wind swirled around, my umbrella turned inside out so many times that I eventually discarded it. The rain became torrential, and when I eventually got back home I was soaked to the skin.

Peeling off my clothes, I could see that the dye from my dress had coloured my skin and the soles of my shoes had fallen off. I turned on the bath taps, hoping for a lovely hot bath only to find that the water was cold.

I sat down and cried.

I understood what this all meant as soon as I woke up. I had been working hard, and instead of my usual meditative periods I had made things hard for myself by making impulsive decisions which had only exacerbated my fatigue.

From that moment on, I never missed out on my meditation, and with a calmer mind was able to make decisions that were positive and health-giving.

Walking across a field, I came face to face with my mother. We talked for a while, and then she said, 'I know I haven't been in touch for some time, but from this moment things will be different.'

Then she kissed me, turned around, and disappeared.

This experience happened soon after I had moved to Spain. I had made the decision to live out there because I was heartbroken by my mother's death and by other events which had torn my life to shreds. About six months later, my late mother appeared in my bedroom, smiled, and then walked out of the door.

When I eventually returned to Britain I visited a

medium, who passed on messages from my mother which forecast my future career as a medium and healer. I could understand her trying to make me into another Harry Edwards; he was a famous healer, and one in whom my mother had placed all her trust when we were ill. But she had always been afraid of the mediumistic side of the psychic world, and that is why I found these messages so strange.

However, another medium passed on a message from my mother at a later date, telling me that she had been wrong to listen to the bigots who tried to defame the reputations of the great mediums of her time. How much proof do we *need* to show that we do progress after death?

Since that time, my mother has been my friend and mentor, and even though there have been periods of between one and three years when I haven't heard from her, when she does come through the messages are powerful, accurate, and immediate.

One night I found myself standing in the door-way of a Buddhist temple. Someone asked me to take off my shoes and handed me a pair of slippers. Then they accompanied me inside the temple, where I was immediately surrounded by Buddhist monks. They began to chant, and as they did so my spirit left my body and I found myself looking down on them. Then I awoke.

This experience was particularly strange, because at the time – the beginning of my mediumistic career when I questioned everything – I had completely turned away from all religious factions. I felt that they were man-made and invented to control the masses. To my mind, spirituality was something you have to earn, not a set of rules that someone else has devised. So I decided to forget this particular journey, feeling that it had no place in my life.

However, over the next few years I received a selection of Buddhist statues from grateful patients. When I asked why they had chosen these particular gifts, they told me that they had no idea – they had simply been drawn to them.

When I wrote my first book *Mind to Mind* years later, I received hundreds of letters from around the world, asking me if I was a Buddhist. It seemed that I had continually referred to Buddhist principles. The same thing happened with every new book I wrote. People sent me books about Buddhism, statues, photographs, and many other gifts appertaining to this belief. They still do.

Today I have a large Buddhist statue in my sitting room and many smaller ones dotted around the house. They seem to instil a sense of peace in me, especially when I am meditating. But to this day, I have never read the books or studied the doctrine. I believe that I have a Buddhist mentor who guides me and who is obviously more enlightened than I am!

I do think there is a great danger in the belief 'the more you know, the more enlightened you become'. I have known hundreds of people who go from one religion to another and who follow the latest New Age doctrines until they become so confused that they forget the most important lesson of all – keep it simple.

There are many books around whose structure is so complicated that by the end the reader cannot remember one single thing that has impressed them. Simplicity is the key to success, no matter what career or hobby you may follow. The same can be said of spiritual matters. Great gifts come in small packages. Faith in the ongoing spirit is all you need; without it, there is no point in this life, or any other.

I was on a sightseeing tour of a huge mansion when I suddenly found myself in a bedroom. Then the curtains began to open and close by themselves. The lights were being switched on and off too, even though it was daylight.

I then found myself running down the stairs, but as I did so I passed a man with a white walking stick. Assuming he was blind, I hurried past him and ran out of the front door into the daylight. But somehow he had got there first. Taking my hand, he said, 'There is no hurry, you will get there in the end.'

I was mystified. Where was I supposed to be going?

This happened at the very beginning of my healing career. I had found myself reluctant to change careers, but everything seemed to work against me until I eventually gave in and began to use the gifts I had inherited from my paternal grandmother. But I had made myself a promise, which was to give it up if I found that cures were not forthcoming. I did not intend to spend the rest of my life on something that would not be exciting and where I might not achieve a certain amount of success. There were too many other things I wanted to do with my life.

At this time I had quite a lot of patients who had varying degrees of blindness, and in some cases I had become frustrated when I could not give quick results, even though they themselves were delighted by the unusual phenomena that followed the healing sessions. For example, they found that bedroom curtains that had been closed at night were open when they awoke, and that the lights in their homes were turned on after they returned home from a healing session. What I didn't realise at the time was that the blind patients who were having these experiences were the ones who would eventually be cured. Later, some of them would see brightly-lit candles, which we all realised was a sign of hope.

This experience gave *me* hope, and eased the enormous pressure that healers sometimes have to endure when undertaking seemingly impossible tasks.

I hope that these experiences will point some of you in the right direction. Awareness is the key to understanding the little things that happen in our lives – and these things are different for everyone because we are all unique.

What soul was his, when, from the naked top
Of some bold headland, he beheld the sun
Rise up, and bathe the world in light!

The Excursion
William Wordsworth 1770–1850

CHAPTER 19

Tunnel Vision

Some people suffer from a physical condition that gives them tunnel vision. From the various descriptions I have been given, it is as though they are looking through a tube, which of course gives them less than the whole picture. Their suffering is great, and they pray for a cure.

But there are also people who suffer a psychological disability which leads to a type of tunnel vision, and it is this kind of disability that I want to examine here, because I believe that 50 per cent of these cases are avoidable. Many of the people I have helped with this disability brought the condition on themselves by spending a lifetime avoiding important issues, refusing to become involved in major decisions, and always assuming that they were right.

We have all met people who refuse to acknowledge the value of any ideas other than their own, and very often the term 'tunnel vision' is applied to them, albeit in a bantering manner. Unfortunately, in very rare cases, they may find that they become victims of the real thing, and the arrogant sufferer cannot believe they have injured themselves in this way.

Obviously it is extremely difficult for doctors to identify when a psychological problem becomes an addiction, for there are some patients in this category who have such an inflated sense of their own importance that they tend to evade issues and blame others for their own unfortunate predicament. Some have problems which are buried deep within their psyche, possibly from childhood, and these are extremely difficult to eradicate.

I treated many patients who had received years of psychiatric counselling which had no effect at all or which had resulted in even more problems. And yet, after just a few months of healing from me, their sight and mental state had improved. So what actually happens in healing that doesn't occur with psychiatric treatment?

The memory bank is stored in the mind, not the brain, which is why people survive death and I receive messages after they have discarded the physical body. Because the mind consists of a structural energy which differs from earthbound energies, it is possible to raise the level of this energy so that it no longer presses on the brain and optic nerves. When this has been accomplished, healing can take place.

Memories actually stay with us from one life to

another, and although bad memories continue to impact on our psyche, there is a stage where this accumulated negativity is discarded. Unless you are suffering, the memories gradually become like distant shadows until your spirituality eliminates them from this life. Regressing people hypnotically to memories of their childhood, and back through the rest of their lives, only reawakens what has happened. It doesn't eliminate any problems – in fact these people are left not only with their current problems to overcome but also with an entirely new set which the mind had buried for them.

I have mentioned this in my books many times over the years, and it has recently been confirmed that this is so by eminent psychiatrists worldwide, especially in cases of trauma victims. I believe that every person who visits a psychiatrist is in some degree of trauma, otherwise they wouldn't be there.

This is why it is essential to have both an open mind and the ability to discuss ideas and emotions – so that the pressure on the mind can be lifted and the normal activity of the brain restored.

One of the reasons for my writing this chapter is to address the terrible trauma suffered by people with tunnel vision, which also affects their families. I have met too many people who refuse to accept any ideas other than their own, and these people disrupt family life to such an extent that their whole family ends up needing counselling. Although I have successfully healed members of such families, in the end they have had to find their own 'free spirit' and learn how to live a more positive and healthy life. Through me, they have also experienced freedom of thought, word and deed, which has inspired them to go on to far greater achievements than they could ever have imagined before healing took place.

I have been able to follow through with many of my patients, and in some cases the results have been astounding. Yet from the beginning there were some who opposed everything I had to say. Such was the faith they had in their own ideas that it was only when their eyesight improved that they gave me the benefit of the doubt. Unfortunately, it was just this kind of egotistical behaviour that caused the problem in the first place. Faith needs to come before the event, not after, for these people to be able to change their habits and go on to healthier thoughts and lifestyles.

Another reason for this kind of tunnel vision is repressing fears that have been so deeply buried within the psyche that the pressure of the mind on the brain damages the optic nerve.

Men are always making jokes about the way women chat to each other, but the joke is on them because it has been scientifically proven that it is the chat that prevents women from experiencing the high level of stress that men suffer. Consequently, no matter what is happening in their psyche, the pressure is periodically released. Because of this, the tunnel vision syndrome occurs more in men than in women.

There are other things that affect the pressure that causes disturbances in vision – partnerships that break up, both in the family and the workplace, because people don't talk to each other. There is a great 'need to know' that exists in all of us, and when we are excluded from something the worry this may cause can build up and up – until it reaches the point of no return – then everyone loses out.

Before you begin to talk to each other, it would be a good idea to polish up your sense of humour. Sometimes a bitter pill is easier to take if there is a smile that can compensate. Remember to be kind to each other and to those around you. We only have this life at the moment, so enjoy it.

I have owed to them,
In hours of weariness, sensations sweet,
Felt in the blood, and felt along the heart;
And passing even into my purer mind,
With tranquil restoration: feelings too
Of unremembered pleasure: such, perhaps,
As have no slight or trivial influence
On that best portion of a good man's life,
His little, nameless, unremembered acts
Of kindness and of love.

Lines Composed a Few Miles Above Tintern Abbey
William Wordsworth 1770–1850

CHAPTER 20

Unkind Acts

It is easy to be unkind; kindness takes effort. That is why there is so much misery in the world.

If children find at an early age that they can make others laugh at the results of their unkind behaviour, they will use this to enhance their popularity. What they don't understand is that the friends they're trying to impress will share the inferiority complex which is at the root of this particular type of victimisation.

It is also a dangerous pursuit, as the victims of malicious acts have been known to commit suicide rather than spend another day being harassed in this way. There are too many children and teenagers suffering these humiliations who believe that suicide is their only way out. I cannot count the number of children brought to me in this condition, and it took a long time to heal their minds so that they could continue their education. Those who do not receive healing and counselling may be left with a bitter hatred of the human race, which can damage their adult lives irrevocably.

Unkind acts are a major problem for society, and as such behaviour becomes more prevalent, so do the depressive illnesses which are brought on by the inhumanity of one person to another. There must be a million or more people a day who are hurt in this way, and yet the perpetrators pass on without a single glance, having carried out what they think of as a clever act.

The type of people who enjoy victimising someone in this way are usually cowards. They need the support of others to back them if the going gets rough, because they don't like to stand alone. There are also people who act in this way because they have themselves been hurt, and so they pass the hurt on to an unsuspecting victim. Unable to live a happy life themselves, they are bent on destroying the happiness of others.

Teenagers are especially vulnerable because of the hormonal changes that are already creating chaos in their minds and bodies. It is at this difficult time, when they are also expected to work hard to reach their potential in their exams, that they most need the love and support of their family and friends. If this is endangered in any way by one unkind person, it can so easily lead to a disastrous outcome, both emotionally in the present and for their future careers. That is why this form of vicious behaviour must be stopped in its tracks before it is too late.

I have heard so many appalling stories from patients whose lives have been made miserable by a family member, friend, or someone at work. Most of these patients were caring and considerate people, but unfortunately these positive traits were the reason they were picked on. Cruel people do not attack their own kind with evil words because they know they would be ignored, so they select the most sensitive to whom the attack will do the most damage.

I have known many famous people. They are sitting targets for those who have failed to get on in life and who are jealous of celebrities' success. Unkind words are used like swords in these circles, and the impact on someone with an artistic and sensitive nature can be devastating. Yet we know that behind these unkind words is a miserable human being – perhaps someone who has been unable to come to terms with his own life and resents those who have managed to make their mark.

Families in particular suffer in this way. If one particular member of a family becomes successful, envy and bitterness may stick in the throats of those who have been unable to fulfil their own dreams. It is then that the snide remarks and unkind actions begin. This kind of mentality eventually becomes an illness, so much so that even if they *do* eventually make their own success, they will still remain warped human beings.

I have seen and heard unbelievably malicious acts perpetrated by children towards their ageing parents when they realised that the financial support they had always received was for some reason no longer available. Instead of taking their turn and supporting the people who gave them life, they disappear from their parents' lives – only to appear again at the reading of the will. I have heard stories of parents permanently separated from their children, who conveniently forgot the years when they were on the receiving end of love, kindness and financial support, and who had cut their parents out of their lives.

Some partners pretend to be kind to their in-laws, when in fact they are deliberately undermining them behind their back. It is extremely difficult to pin down a perpetual liar, but if partners could only be courageous enough to get the family together and really sort out the truth from the lies by giving everyone involved the chance to speak, then the perpetrator would be exposed and many families would be reunited.

As we grow up, we should make the most of the time spent with our parents. When they die, it is too late to say 'sorry'. I have seen the pain that has overcome so many people when they have come to me for healing after a parent has died. They have been unable to deal with the guilt they feel when they remembered how badly they had treated that parent. Some of these people were so distraught that they asked me if I could contact their dead parent so that they could ask for their forgiveness. But mediumship does not work in this way. The contact has to come from the deceased. In many cases, however, this connection was initiated by the deceased at a later date.

Those who cannot resist making unkind remarks should think very carefully about the future. One way or another, their behaviour will come back to haunt them. They should think about their own mental and physical health. Unkind thoughts create havoc within the mind and body, and chaotic thought becomes the norm. They will lose all sense of right and wrong, and – unable to differentiate truth from lies – they become the victims of their own maliciousness.

People who have not been on the receiving end of this type of misery may think that the word 'unkind' does not appear to carry such a terrible stigma as 'cruel', but I believe they are one and the same thing. No matter how much someone may think that their unkind actions towards their parents will not affect their own lives, I can assure you that they will. The mind holds memories that cannot be erased – memories of all the kindness they received from their parents as they were growing up, the shelter they were provided with until they were able to strike out on their own, and even then, the support they were given if anything went wrong. And the mind reminds them that instead of returning this kindness, these people have used the strength they had in the prime of their lives to persecute the very people who *gave* them that strength. This is a major crime, and the Western world is full of these heartless people. Anyone who causes a rift between family members should realise that their crime, and the abject misery it has caused to those involved, will never be forgotten.

There are, of course, children who undoubtedly had a miserable childhood, who think that their parents don't deserve any help. But this is too easy. Blood is thicker than water, and there is nothing to stop these young people giving help, if only to show that they are made of kinder stuff. They will reap the rewards later, as 'what one gives out will return'.

The whole world is being made ill by the cruel actions and words that are heaped upon unsuspecting and innocent victims. And it can happen anywhere at any time. One moment you are at peace with the world, and then someone cuts your heart out. It is as simple as that.

If this chapter has made anyone feel guilty, then please do something about it! It is never too late to build bridges – or to rebuild those which should never have been broken in the first place.

PART FOUR

*Proof of Interaction
Between Mind and Body*

A thing of beauty is a joy for ever:
Its loveliness increases; it will never
Pass into nothingness; but still will keep
A bower quiet for us, and a sleep
Full of sweet dreams, and health, and quiet breathing.

Endymion
John Keats 1795–1821

CHAPTER 21

Exercise and Yoga

This chapter is not meant to be an authority on yoga but rather an aid for those who have never attempted yoga exercises before. I will take you through some simple exercises that will help you to maintain your mind, body and spirit. The secret of yoga is to take things slowly. I cannot emphasise too much the need for vigilance in this respect – I have seen too many disastrous results of people doing too much, too soon.

The problem with beginners' classes is that they try to keep in step with everyone else. Our bodies are our temples, and over time the building blocks will begin to crumble and break down. It is usually at this point that someone will make the decision to do something about it and begin their search for eternal youth. But believe me, there is no such thing. What we *can* do, however, is use gentle exercise and breathing techniques that can prevent further damage and thus delay the ageing process.

Human beings come in all shapes and sizes, and

that's how it should be, otherwise we'd look like androids! The first step is to love your body, no matter what state it is in. If you don't, others will take their cue from you and disrespect who you are.

Begin this process by trying to avoid looking into the mirror as much as usual. Mirrors do not reflect the inner beauty or the mind – nor do they show up the laughter lines that are so attractive when we smile, because we don't usually smile when we look at our reflections. Instead, all we see is a miserable-looking individual staring back at us. This may trigger a depressive reaction which can ruin the whole day!

Another depressing and futile act is to stand on the scales every day. We all have varying degrees of water retention that may negate any weight loss we have made from our yoga. Keep off the scales for a month and use a tape measure instead, or occasionally try on clothes that you haven't been able to get into for some time.

If you indulge in any kind of rigorous exercise, your weight will actually increase as the muscle power returns, for as the fat burns up, it leaves pockets which fill with water until the tissues shrink and eliminate the water retention. But the tape measure never lies, and you will find that your measurements will shrink as your body tightens up, no matter what the scales may tell you. If the tape measurements do not alter in your favour, then you need to adjust your diet and exercise routine until you achieve a positive result (assuming that you are trying to trim down – not everyone needs to, of course).

If you are disabled you should continually move those parts of the body that can take gentle exercise because this will improve the circulation to both body and brain. If you are taking medicinal drugs, perhaps these are creating weight problems you can do nothing about. You should not despair however, for there are other benefits from yoga that can bring about a transformation.

You must never forget that the mind needs to be exercised in conjunction with the body. You should try to keep negative thoughts at bay and concentrate on the positive aspects of your life. It isn't always easy to do this, but it's a necessity if you wish to turn your life around.

Meditation brings peace and relaxation. You will be freeing your mind from its eternal prison and taking pressures off the body so that it can release the blockages which affect all the major organs. You may find some help in Chapter 17 on daydreaming.

Don't set your sights too high, otherwise you will be disappointed. Think, if you lose just one pound per week, that's 52 pounds a year, or just under four stone. Which overweight people wouldn't be satisfied with that result? On that kind of regime you can even indulge in a few of your favourite foods.

The best kind of diet would consist of fresh whole foods, plenty of fruit and vegetables, fish, a little meat, and a variety of other foods like pasta – with that lot, you will hardly become bored with eating the same old thing. Salads are always being promoted as the most marvellous means to lose weight, and they are an excellent source of vitamins and minerals, but there are thousands of people who do not care for them. If you don't like salad, replace it with any raw fruit and vegetables that you *do* like. It is important not to have any guilt when embarking on a diet, so if you choose intelligently and carefully, you can have it all – weight loss *and* food satisfaction.

If you follow the easy exercises in this chapter, you will notice an improvement in your posture, vision and general appearance, and with a clearer skin, you will start to look young again. In fact, I have seen extremely overweight people who have attracted a lot of compliments by simply having a good complexion.

Yoga deals with the whole – with physical, mental and spiritual growth. As you continue to follow this regime you will be aware of a power building up inside you as the chakras – the energy centres – open up and draw in even more life force. But there are a few rules you will have to remember, so copy them out and pin them to the wall in the room in which you choose to exercise.

1. Always practise the exercises on a empty stomach.
2. Choose an airy, well-ventilated room.
3. For the first week, do not exercise more than fifteen minutes a day.
4. Always practise the deep breathing method whilst doing the exercises. Breathe in as you go into the postures, and breathe out when you return. If you can't do this at first, just keep breathing normally until you can. (Holding your breath will do you no good at all!)
5. Do not wear tight clothes, because this will constrict you whilst you are doing the postures.
6. Rest frequently between the exercises. If you feel tired at the end of each session, do less until you feel comfortable with your efforts.
7. Strenuous exercises should never be undertaken by pregnant women without the doctor's consent.
8. Above all, use your common sense. It will always stand you in good stead!

Stretching Exercises

Begin your day by doing some stretching exercises as soon as you wake up. While still in bed, yawn several times, stretch your arms and legs, and then stretch your whole body.

The next step is to swing your legs over the side of the bed, relax, and then stand up. Never jump straight out of bed – this will shock the system, which is the last thing you want before you start the day.

If you study animals, you will see that they yawn and stretch before they get to their feet. Studying nature in all its forms is an excellent way of picking up new ideas for optimum health.

You should always give yourself time to practise some simple breathing techniques in the morning before you eat. So why not get up a little earlier than normal to carry out these exercises?

Breathing Exercises

Sit in an upright chair to support the spine, neck and head, put your hands on your knees and close your eyes. Breathe in by slightly contracting the back wall of the mouth, drawing air through the nose so that you will hear a hissing noise. The lower ribs should expand first, and then the rest. The beginner should not try to take in too much air at any one time, just practise the breathing technique until you are comfortable with the sensation. At first, inhale to the count of three, hold the breath for two counts, and then slowly exhale. The chest and shoulders should always remain motionless. You will need to use a little pressure to push the air out, and the hissing noise will be less apparent. Remember when you exhale that the upper ribs are contracted first, the exact opposite of when you inhale.

You'll soon get the hang of it, because if you breathe in through the nose without contracting the back of the mouth, there will be no hissing noise, and you will only be able to take in air in very small quantities, certainly not enough to expand the ribs.

As you continue to practise, raise the inhaling and exhaling counts until you feel that you have reached your limit. Do not go beyond your personal limit, no matter how many people boast about their own achievements. We are all different, and – as individuals – exercise our own judgement in these matters in an intelligent manner. The most important thing to remember is to extend your breathing abilities every day. After a week or so, you'll be surprised at how much better you will feel.

When you become adept, you will be able to go on to the next step. Put your fingers on your wrist and inhale to the count of your pulse, then exhale in the same way. If you wish to pause between the beats, then do so, until you get into the swing of things. This is a fantastic exercise for those who suffer with palpitations because it acts as a control.

Sometimes, at the first reading, it is difficult to absorb and retain instruction, but don't let this deter you. If you just start with the breathing techniques, they will calm your mind and improve your memory until you find that you can absorb information like a sponge!

Later, when your life force centres open up, the extra energy will stimulate every cell in your body.

Eye Exercises

Sometimes bad eyesight can be the result of the muscles around the eye becoming lazy through lack of exercise. In most cases our neck is doing too much work. For instance, when you look up, the head goes back and the eyes stay as they were. They hardly move at all. The correct thing would be to make only a slight movement of the head and let the eyes do the rest. The same thing happens if you want to look sideways. We turn our heads so that our eyes are in a direct line with what we want to look at, instead of a slight turn and a strong eye movement.

It is extremely difficult to get out of the bad habits of a lifetime, so the following exercises are intended to help you to use the eye muscles in a controlled way, to strengthen and improve your sight.

Sit in an upright chair, keeping your spine straight, and place your hands on your knees. Now look up as far as you can without moving your head, pause for a minute, then reverse this action by looking down at a point on the ground. Relax, then repeat the exercise four times.

Remember to keep the whole body still at all

times. Also, these exercises must be done very slowly, because the eyes will move easily once the muscles have tightened.

Without straining your eyes, look to your right, pause, and then look to your left, pause, and then look ahead. Relax.

Next, look up at the right hand corner of your eyes, pause, and then look down to the left hand corner. Relax. Then reverse this process so that you look up at the left hand corner and then down to the right hand corner. Then relax.

Remember to carry out each individual exercise four times. Don't extend this until your eyesight improves – you don't want to strain your eyes.

The following instruction should only be practised when you have perfected all of the moves mentioned thus far.

Slowly roll your eyes clockwise, then anti-clockwise. Look up, and then look down.

To change your vision from close to distant points, place your finger on the tip of your nose, then gradually move it away in a straight line until you have reached a position where it is still clear, then raise your eyes, and look into the distance. When you have repeated this several times, close your eyes and squeeze them tight.

If you practise this exercise every day, it will undoubtedly improve your sight.

Arm-strengthening Exercise

Stand directly in front of a wall and then move back a little. Your legs should be apart, in line with your shoulders. Place your outstretched arms against the wall, lining them up with your shoulders at shoulder height. Then with your palms flat against the wall, push yourself back and forth. These are push-ups but in the upright position. Start by doing them four times, twice a day, and increase until you reach your maximum without stress.

This exercise is excellent for those who find it difficult to walk. It helps circulation and strengthens the arms, which need to be strong to use aids such as crutches and wheelchairs. If standing is also a problem, ask someone to support your back whilst you exercise.

To stretch the back of your legs at the same time, do the press-ups against a piece of furniture or table.

Palming

This exercise has an extremely beneficial effect on the nervous system. Make yourself comfortable by sitting in an upright chair at a table and place your elbows on the table. In order to reach a point where you feel totally relaxed, you may need to rest them on a couple of books. Experiment until you feel totally at ease with your position.

The next step is to rub your hands together, to charge them with electricity, and then place your cupped hands over your closed eyes. The fingers of the right hand should be placed over the fingers of your left hand, in the middle of the forehead, with the thumbs drawn into the sides of the eyes and face. This should block out every speck of light so that you are in total darkness.

This exercise will help those who find it difficult to 'let go' and allow their mind to be free, because it completely shuts out the outside world as you enter a state of complete relaxation.

I have heard the most extraordinary stories from clients who have tried palming. Most of them have been able to see colours in their true light, and many have seen their deceased family and friends appearing on the black screen of their mind. Pets appear regularly. Others see amazing kaleidoscopic patterns.

You will never know what you will see until you try. At the very least, you will be bringing harmony and balance to your mind, body and spirit.

Yoga Postures

In this section I will only be describing the easy postures. If you find that they have a beneficial effect on your health, then you may want to find a Wheel of Yoga teacher. It is important that you seek out the best, so check that they are registered.

The Rocking Posture

This is an excellent posture with which to start the day as it limbers up the spine. It is certainly a fantastic anti-ageing posture, because a flexible spine is the finest way to maintain a youthful appearance. If you suffer from insomnia, then this is also a must before you go to bed at night, because it will help you to sleep more soundly.

If you have an exercise mat or something similar, then place this on the floor. Otherwise use several bath towels until you can find the right piece of equipment.

Sit down on the end of the mat, then draw your knees up and bend your head forward. Now put your hands under your knees. If you can join your hands at this point, then do so, but if you can't it doesn't matter: it will all become easier with time. Keeping your spine in a rounded position, you are now ready to rock back and forth like a rocking chair. Don't go too slowly or you'll land on your back. If this happens, just laugh at yourself and try again. I cannot emphasise too much that you are not in competition with anyone. You will always be in control of your own regime. If there are some days when you don't feel like exercising, then don't. When you are in this frame of mind, the body stiffens as it receives the negative messages from your mind. When you feel inclined to try again, then you will have restored the positive reactions and your body will work for you.

You may find that if you straighten your knees as you go back, and bend them again as you swing forward, it will be easier for you to maintain rhythm.

This is a wonderful posture, because no matter what state your body may be in, you can adjust it to your capabilities. I have known people whose spines were so stiff they were unable to do this easy exercise at first. But with perseverance, and taking it slowly so as not to strain their muscles, they were eventually able to achieve miraculous results. Many of them found that their health improved so much that they went on to become qualified yoga teachers themselves.

Remember, always keep within the safety boundaries of your own unique body. If you feel pain, relax and come back until you are in a comfortable position.

This posture releases blockages along the spinal cord and in the meridian lines (energy channels), and stimulates the central nervous system.

The Cobra Pose

You will find this exercise comparatively easy if you have been able to successfully practise the Rocking Posture.

Lie down on your stomach with your chin touching the floor. Place the palms of both hands on the exercise mat whilst keeping the elbows above the floor. Then breathe in as you gently raise your head, shoulders, chest and upper body, whilst keeping the lower part of your body on the mat. Your elbows should remain bent at all times. Begin to exhale whilst gently lowering your body until your chin touches the floor again. If you feel too much pressure in the lower part of the back, take the upper body to a point where it feels more comfortable. Some people find it difficult even to raise their elbows at first. If this is the case, then strengthen your arms by following the Arm-strengthening Exercise.

The adrenal glands will become more active, enabling them to send a richer supply of blood to the kidneys. Adjustments in the spinal column will benefit those of you who suffer with lower back pain. And it is an excellent aid for women who suffer from ovarian and uterine problems.

If you have never done any yoga before, it would be a good idea to start with the breathing, neck and eye exercises. When you are comfortable with these, you can then go on to the next step. It is essential, however, that you do not push yourself to a point where you feel tired when you have finished the exercises. Instead, you should feel completely relaxed and at ease with the renewed balance of your mind and body.

Yoga positions have been designed to exercise

every part of the body and to open the chakras in the energy system, enabling them to draw in more life force to sustain the physical body. The instructions given in this chapter may give the impression that the postures are fairly simple, and therefore easy. This will soon evaporate once you start on your new regime! But your body will tell you how much work you will have to do on strengthening your mind in order to get good results. You will find this a real eye-opener.

Balance is the key to success. Our immune system relies on this balance to keep disease at bay and to maintain a healthy system. That is why the energy counterpart – with its meridian lines and chakras – has to be the first to change, before it can manifest on the physical.

The following exercises are for those of you who now find the first postures easy.

The Raised Leg Posture

Lie down on your back with your hands along the sides of your body. Take a deep breath, whilst raising your right leg at right angles to your body. Stay in this position for a minute or two without bending the knee and while keeping your left leg flat against the floor. Then exhale while slowly lowering the leg.

Repeat this process with the left leg.

The next step is to raise both legs at the same

time – this is usually the difficult bit – wait a few seconds, and then lower them. To begin with, you should only practise this twice a day. Then after a few days of raising and lowering your legs, you will begin to feel more comfortable and more adept.

This exercise gives internal massage, which will strengthen the muscles and reduce fat. It's great for a flabby tummy!

If you have a weak heart, or suffer from gynaecological problems, you should not attempt this exercise without referring to your doctor.

The Lotus Posture

I expect many of you will have heard of the Lotus Position, even if you have never tried yoga before. Again, this posture has to be taken slowly, and you must never try to force it. It doesn't matter if you can only do a small part of the exercise at first, because it is better than nothing.

Sit on the floor and place the sole of your left foot against the inside of your right thigh. Then, gently pressing down on your left knee, slowly get into a rhythmic bouncing motion. This action will stretch and limber up ligaments that have become rigid with lack of use. The muscles will also benefit, and when all of these things have come together, you will find this exercise easy. However, I doubt that your knee will touch the floor for some time, but as long as you can feel the pull in your thigh you are on the right track. If you feel pain, stop, and be more gentle with yourself.

To begin with, you might find it easier to place the left foot *on* the right thigh, instead of against it.

When you feel comfortable with this exercise, you can go onto the next step of the Lotus Position by placing the right foot on the left thigh. Bounce the right knee as before, until it reaches the floor, then bend your left knee, take the left foot with both hands and slide it over the right leg, bringing it to rest on right thigh. If you can do this, you will now be sitting in the Lotus Position. This is a great achievement. It doesn't matter if it takes you a year to get to this stage. When you do it it is a great feeling!

Still in this position, place the hands on the knees, with the palms open and facing out. The thumb and second finger on each hand should be touching, forming an O. This is the sign for OM, which is the most famous and most used mantra of all.

The Lotus Position calms the mind and the nervous system. It is a classical yoga pose and is used for concentration and meditation.

This chapter has been simply a 'Starter Pack', and has been designed to enable the reader to try some of the simpler exercises and yoga positions without becoming too involved in the deeper meanings of yoga – this can come later. If you do want to dig deeper and go on to the more difficult postures, then you will need to find a good teacher. You should not go any further along this path without proper tuition.

I introduced my family to yoga about 50 years ago. Through perseverance and commitment, my daughter Janet became a Wheel of Yoga teacher, until her natural talents as a medium and healer surfaced. It is impossible to separate these gifts, as inspiration and intelligence come from the same source.

If any reader finds health, happiness, peace and a spiritual path having followed the exercises in this chapter, then my efforts will not have been in vain.

I hope that all of your dreams will be fulfilled, helping you to walk through life with your head held high so that your vision of the future will not be impaired.

If a little knowledge is dangerous, where is the man who has so much as to be out of danger?

T. H. Huxley 1825–1895

CHAPTER 22

Hand Analysis

I have been fascinated with the configurations of lines on the palms of the hands for as long as I can remember. Before I became a professional medium and healer, I was always secretly analysing the lines on the hands of family and friends, as well as those of perfect strangers. A raised hand to the face would immediately bring out the 'detective' in me.

Fifty years ago I was pursuing a singing career, so my time was limited. But it was in the rest periods between rehearsals that my gift for hand reading was put to good use. In fact, so many people were fascinated with the results of my analysis that they asked me if I would see them on a regular basis. I agreed to do this, provided they limited the sessions to once every three months, as it takes time for the lines and patterns on the hand to change.

Analysing hands not only eased the boredom, but it filled that spare time with laughter as I added a bit of humour to the readings. To this day, I believe that no matter what method you use to give a reading, the subject is more likely to accept the truth if it is given with a smile. Taking yourself too seriously is a sure way to lose friends and to attract depression. I don't know one person who hasn't got a cross to bear, but that's life. Whether we like it or not, we're stuck with it, and it is entirely our choice if we make mountains out of molehills or vice versa – and I would suggest the latter!

There were times when I saw something in the hand that seemed to be at odds with the personality, but as I grew more adept, it became clear to me that I had been looking into the future.

But, I hear you ask, if the lines on the hand change as a result of the interaction between the mind and the hands, how can one see something that has not yet happened? The answer is simple. Changes are occurring in our subconscious long before we become aware of those changes. Therefore the lines will appear before rather than after the event.

To a competent analyst the hands are like an open book, its author the subject of the reading. Indeed, hand analysis becomes a lifelong interest once you have been hooked, and the hook that grips you is very often correctly diagnosing your first pairs of hands.

Amateur palmists tend to look at the length of the life line as an indication of longevity. This obvious assumption is wrong. A short but deep life line also gives an indication of longevity, but it is necessary to look at other aspects of the hands in order to substantiate this.

I was looking at the palm of a patient while giving her healing, and I noticed that she had a very short life line. Aware that I was paying rather a lot of attention to this, she told me that when she was only 20 years old a palmist had told her that she would not have a long life. I was appalled that anyone reading palms should have made such a dangerously negative remark. Fortunately, the lady in question was extremely intelligent, and had only thought about the prediction when she'd suffered minor setbacks with her health. But she did admit that she'd never thought that she would ever live to retirement age. She was now 80!

Fortunately, I was able to reassure her that she still had a lot more time left and would live her life to the full, because the rest of her hand was indicative of someone who had possessed – and still did to some extent – an amazing vitality. She was 98 when she died.

A short and shallow lifeline shows that the necessary vitality needed for a healthy life is lacking, but this can be turned around by paying special attention to lifestyle and dietary needs. I would also urge someone with this type of life line to take extra vitamins and minerals, and to take plenty of exercise. You can easily turn a negative into a positive, and this will show up in the life line as the health improves.

The wonderful thing about the interaction between the mind and body is that we can always reverse the negative with the power of the mind. Even the breaks that occur in the life line, and which amateur palmists might read as a serious illness or accident, cannot be taken out of context. Other lines must be investigated – especially the heart line – if you are to give an accurate diagnosis.

A common sign at the beginning of a life line is a configuration called a chain, and it does indeed look like a chain. This usually points to difficulties at birth, or a sign of delicate health at that time. If it occurs in the middle of a life line, then it suggests a debility in the energy system. Once again, the positive outcome should be that you pay attention to your health and try not to become involved in stressful situations. Peace and happiness are the best cure for this sign.

The heart line is the uppermost line on the hand, nearest the base of the fingers. This is the second most significant line, so it is important to relate it to findings on the life line when making a diagnosis. This line reflects the emotional upheavals within our lives, and also the functional disorders appertaining to the vital organ from which it takes its name.

One word of warning: you should never reach a diagnosis with respect to heart disease on the reading of this line alone. Indeed, if there are indications that there may be something wrong – when the other lines have also been taken into consideration – the palmist should suggest that the subject seek medical advice, if only to put their mind at rest. No one should try to play God.

One interesting fact about the heart line is that palmists can detect the necessity for the sitter to have their eyes tested. I have found that a small island under the base of the third finger can indicate a weakness in this area, and over the years I have never known this sign to be wrong.

It requires great expertise to read the heart line, because the small faint lines that appear and disappear with regularity are the emotional upsets that we all experience through life. These small lines are indicative of the interaction between the mind and the body.

If the heart line stops beneath the base of the second finger – which is called Saturn – the subject's love life will be greatly influenced by sensuality. People who practise self-induced stimulation, whether sexual or through drugs and drink, are often found to have a line above the heart line called 'the girdle of Venus'. This usually rises between the index finger, namely Jupiter, and forms a full or half arc beneath either Saturn, third finger Apollo, or little finger Mercury. If the girdle has a double line, or one that is broken up, it can indicate a hysterical temperament. But if it is seen on a normal or artistic hand, it can be an indication of heightened awareness. That is why it is important to look at the hand as a whole and not to make any diagnosis on small sections that may not be upheld in the other characteristics.

The third major line in the hand is the head line. This normally originates between the thumb and index finger, above the beginning of the life line. If the space between the two at this point is a definite separation, it is a sign of individuality and a desire for independence. Health troubles, mental and physical, show up either as islands, as the chained effect, or if the line is broken or split in any way.

There is another line, the Simian line, so-called because it resembles the single line found in the hands of monkeys. This runs in a straight line across the palm, replacing both the heart and head lines. Much has been written about this line, and a diagnosis should never be made by amateurs because the Simian line has a distinctly negative side. Conversely, it has also been found in the hands of devoutly religious and creative personalities. Professionals would certainly study the formation of the thumb before reaching any conclusions.

One of the negative aspects of the Simian line is the fixations that these people may have throughout their lives which can create havoc within themselves and those around them. That is why it is important, in all hand analysis, to take into account the positive aspects of the type of hand, so that the sitter can try to strengthen that part of the character and thus lessen the impact of the negative.

It is interesting to note that there are people in governments all around the world who have a Simian line!

Secondary Lines

The line of fate can start from the base of the hand, from the life line, from the mount of Luna (the pad at the edge of the hand opposite the thumb) or rom the centre of the hand, and always ends on the mount of Saturn, the small pad under the second finger.

If someone does not have a line of fate, this can be significant, because its presence represents emotional maturity and adaptability. Patients have often been referred to me by doctors unable to establish emotional contact with their patient. In every case, the line of fate was absent. Although the patients themselves were happy individuals, content with a simple life, their families found them difficult to deal with because of their inability to take on any kind of responsibility.

A person who has a double fate line, especially if it is broken, is liable to suffer illnesses brought about by their inability to wed reality to their need for spirituality. If they bury this need by pursuing materialistic gain, their health will deteriorate.

Knowing about the negativity of the lines can help the palmist to turn the sitter's attention to strengthening the positive aspects of their hands. Chains in any of the lines signifies weakness. Some illnesses show up as short chains which start to fade when the illness has passed. If a fate line is chained from beginning to end, it signifies that the individual will experience career problems all their life. But as always there is a positive alternative – to choose a simpler lifestyle. Then the struggle will not be so hard.

Islands that appear on the line of fate, especially if they are near the base of the hand, usually denote emotional insecurity in one or both parents before the child was born. But if the child is mentally and physically strong, the rest of the line will be normal, as their own psyche takes over.

The ability to read one's own hand in this way can make life a whole lot easier to bear. Remember, the mind is the hand that drew the map in the first instance, and it will continue to do so throughout your life. Making a study of your own hands will keep you up to date with what is going on in your subconscious.

The line of Apollo has no particular starting point in the hand but usually runs in the general direction of the Mount of Apollo, the small pad beneath the ring finger. As in all the lines, the length and quality of the secondary lines are important, because the palmist would read these in conjunction with the major lines.

The line of Apollo is especially indicative of the talent and success of the individual, and a strong line will show a leaning towards creativity in the arts. When this line is broken up, the talent will take a back seat until the need to exercise it returns.

The absence of this line does not necessarily mean that the person does not have artistic leanings. Indeed, in the hand of a genius it is often missing. Here, the secret of success has been in the length, depth and direction of the fate line, which usually starts at the 'bracelet' on the wrist.

With talented musicians, I have seen a small dash in the Apollo area, although the fate lines have been completely unbroken, indicating that their musical career had been determined from birth.

If there is an island on the line of Apollo, the subject must exercise caution with regard to material gains and should not take this aspect of life for granted. What is gained can just as easily be lost.

The line of Mercury usually starts in the middle of the palm and ends on the mount of Mercury underneath the little finger. This line is not as well defined as the other lines in the hand and is often absent.

However, if it is well defined it can mean that the subject is extremely robust in an earthy way. Medical hand analysts would pay a great deal of attention to the line of Mercury, as it is the line of health. Because of this, special consideration should be made to other aspects in the hand before attempting a diagnosis.

Subordinate Signs

Some palmists pay particular attention to subordinate signs, but I have found that they are not foolproof and therefore, as a medical hand analyst, I would always look elsewhere in the hand for confirmation.

Most of the signs listed below negate the positive aspects of a line, but there are one or two features, like the island and the chain, that I have found to be particularly significant. There are palmists who think they are all significant, but as this chapter is only an introduction to palmistry I will not give a detailed account of each one – for that you will need to consult a book by a professional hand analyst.

1. Cross
2. Star
3. Square
4. Circle
5. Island

6. Grille
7. Fork
8. Triangle
9. Chain
10. Dot

The Fingers

The thumb and fingers of both hands need to be examined carefully as part of any diagnosis. Before analysing the fingers, it is necessary to determine whether they are long or short. This can be done by closing the fingers and folding them over the palm. If they cover most of the palm they can be considered long; if they only come halfway to the wrist, they would be short. Extremely long fingers can reach the 'bracelet' lines on the wrist.

Long fingers indicate a person who tends to be preoccupied with detail to such an extent that they become distracted by small things to the exclusion of the whole. Thin fingers suggest a suspicious or nervous personality, whereas a subject with thick fingers will be less inclined to have nervous reactions to everyday problems.

Prominent knuckles on long thin fingers show an aspect of the personality that may exasperate others. These people tend to deliberate for far too long over small details; they may also be extremely stubborn.

If the knuckles are smooth, the subject will be

less analytical and tends to lean towards a more spiritual life.

Short fingers indicate the complete opposite. These people show little regard for detail and always try to look at the whole picture. Acting on impulse, this type of personality can easily become temporarily neurotic because of a tendency to over-react. Their inability to concentrate on menial tasks can affect their career.

As always, there is hope, and this lies is in the tips of the fingers. Pointed fingers are an indication that the person has a lively imagination, and this can save them from the most negative aspects of the fingers. Square tips indicate someone who studies facts in a reasonable manner and who is not judgmental about emotional or materialistic issues.

The first finger, the index finger or finger of Jupiter, links the individual with the material environment. An extremely short index finger would indicate low self esteem and an inferiority complex. To gauge whether the finger is long or short, it should be measured against the other fingers. A normal index finger will reach the middle of the first phalange, or section, of the middle finger, Saturn. If, however, it is shorter than the ring finger, Apollo, it would be considered as short.

Those with a short index finger are modest and avoid making themselves conspicuous in any way. A long index finger, extending beyond the ring finger, will belong to someone who is exceedingly ambitious. I have seen many pairs of hands where someone has one long index finger and one much shorter, which indicates that the psyche is balanced.

The finger of Saturn balances both the conscious and unconscious mind. It has a steadying influence on the personality, especially if there are other signs in the hand that indicate someone with a reckless nature.

A long Saturn finger is one that extends beyond both the index and Apollo. A short finger shows that the person might be lacking in self-control and tends to take risks. These tendencies can be overcome, but the hand would have to be studied carefully before reaching a conclusion.

The finger of Apollo, the ring finger, is linked with creativity and intuition. It is often referred to as the Sun finger because of its affinity with the arts. A long ring finger would be longer than the index finger, and an extremely long ring finger indicates a personality who is highly imaginative, someone who is content with their own company.

However, if the ring finger is shorter than the index finger, it could indicate that the subject has such a desire to be recognised that they harbour an exaggerated view of their own capabilities.

The length of the little finger, Mercury, can be established by comparing it to the ring finger. A normal length would reach the line between the upper and second sections of that finger. A long Mercury finger would go beyond that point, and a short one would fail to reach it.

If the finger of Mercury stands apart from the ring finger, it can signify problems in personal relationships. If the finger is set low on the hand, so that the base is not aligned with the other fingers, this can indicate a parent fixation. If this finger is twisted in any way, it signifies a person who enjoys getting under the skins of others. This is an unpleasant trait, and those who are afflicted with it should work hard to curb it.

The Mercury finger is closely associated, amongst other things, with sensual and sexual appetites. It's a finger to be reckoned with, and anyone making a diagnosis on this finger alone would need to treat it carefully.

The thumb has always been regarded as the most important part of the hand. It signifies vitality, will and self-expression. If an individual hides their thumb, this may indicate a state of anxiety and insecurity. It is also an indication of dependency. A straight, rigid thumb points to someone with drive and determination, but with a certain rigidity in their mental attitude towards life in general. The flexible thumb denotes versatility and the ability to 'go with the flow'.

The length of the thumb is extremely important. A thumb of average length when held against the side of the hand will reach mid-way up the bottom phalange of the index finger. If it fails to reach this point it would be considered short, whereas a long thumb will go past the first phalange. The larger the thumb, the greater the energy.

When examining the thumb, it is important to look at the nail section first. If this is larger than the second joint, then the subject will possess great determination and willpower. If it is shorter, then it will denote someone who has a 'laid-back' attitude to life. A clubbed nail phalange shows an inclination towards violence.

If the second phalange has a narrow, waisted look, it would indicate an individual with superior intelligence. If it is thick, it is a sign of impulsive behaviour. If it is flat, there could be some constitutional weakness and a lack of nervous energy.

If the first and second sections of the thumb are of equal length, it denotes a strong willpower and sound judgement. If the second section is dominant, then that person may lack the necessary attributes to carry through on important issues and may be someone who acts without thinking things through. The most desirable thumb is one where the two sections are of more or less equal length, which balances the whole.

Palmists nearly always read the right hand first, because most people are right-handed and this hand usually shows the stronger lines. There has always been controversy between palmists over whether this should still stand if the person is left-handed. I have always maintained that if a person is left-handed – and this does have a connection with the brain – then that hand will have more configurations. I am left-handed, and having studied my own hands throughout my life, I have found this to be true.

When I was young, I was forced to write with my right hand at school. This caused a lot of difficulties – emotional and practical – because I was unable to write with any speed. But when I was ten a law was passed that protected children from this kind of abuse in school and stopped them from being traumatised in this way.

I believe that this shows without doubt the effect that both the waking and the subconscious mind have on the hands, because these small traumas can still be seen in my own hands.

I'd like to return to the mystery of how the subconscious mind affects the markings on the hand. Pictures of unborn babies in the womb show that the majority have clenched fists. It is this pressure that writes the major lines found in the palms of newborn babies. Time and time again, parents have asked me to read the hands of their tiny babies, to help them to treat their child as a unique individual. I was able to give them details of the kind of personality their child had inherited and advice on how to handle the child in the first years of its life.

As I was able to follow through with these children, I found that the readings were not only accurate but that the character and personality diagnoses had been correct too. The parents of the babies assured me that these first readings had been invaluable because it had enabled those with more than one child in the family to treat them all as individuals. The children consequently grew up knowing just who they were and had the courage to follow their own stars.

A reading from a professional hand analyst is not the kind of reading that you would get from a five-minute fairground palmist. It is a thorough investigation of every line, every fingerprint, the shape of the hands and fingers, etc. A record should be kept of the prints so that each reading can be compared with the previous one. Changes in attitude, lifestyle and health can be immediately identified, and if there are any signs of negativity the analyst would point them out and give the appropriate counselling.

It is amazing how the lines of the hand change when someone enters into a new relationship. If a reading is made of the hands of both partners, before and after, they will clearly show how the characteristics of each partner have made an impression on the other with the addition of minor identical lines. It is also easy to see whether the relationship will be successful or not. But when people are in love – or lust – they usually ignore any advice if they are happy with what is going on in their lives. (This is a fairly normal reaction!)

If we are going to improve in character and personality, it is sometimes necessary to experience the bad along with the good. How else are we to learn? It is only when an analyst recognises that the new lines are destructive that they try to turn the situation around, and they can do this with ease, by giving a logical explanation to an illogical problem. When this works it can give you a great sense of fulfilment.

Your hands are your life maps, and the mistakes of the past – so clearly written at one time – will become fainter as soon as the problems have gone from your mind.

But some aspects of your hands never change – your fingerprints. Unless there has been any external physical damage, we die with the same formations on the tips of our fingers that we were born with. They are unique to each individual, and no two sets of fingerprints can ever be the same. You may think that identical twins might have identical fingerprints, but even this is not the case.

Fingerprints must surely be the only thing in this world that never changes. That is why they are used by the police and forensic scientists to help them identify criminals and unidentified bodies. No one has yet been able to solve the mystery of unique fingerprints, but I believe they are soul patterns, for the mind/soul of every individual is also unique.

The types of fingerprint patterns found on the tips of the fingers are:

1. Loop
2. Tented Arch
3. Arch (lower than Tented Arch)
4. Whorl
5. Composite

The Loop can run from left to right or vice versa. It indicates someone with a versatile character and endearing personality.

The Tented Arch resembles the middle pole of a tent, high in the centre and flowing down each side. There is a certain amount of nervous disability connected to this pattern, which is present in those of an artistic or visionary nature. These people should always seek peace and harmony, as they would find life difficult to bear if they were surrounded by noise and strife.

The Arched pattern looks like a little hill. The centre may not be well defined. A secretive pattern, it often belongs to a repressive personality who could at times have destructive tendencies. These people are often resentful and suspicious, and lead a solitary life. Thankfully, most people tend to have only one or two Arched fingerprints and are therefore balanced.

The Whorl is exactly how it sounds – a whirlpool. It shows an individualistic, independent and determined person, but one who would be a congenial companion.

The Composite print – two or more different patterns – shows a materialistic mind, lack of elasticity, and a critical and overbearing personality.

Having studied medical hand analysis for many years, I decided to specialise in this field. It was essential to my study of vitamin and mineral therapy, because the lack of these substances are clearly shown in the hand. Later, it was to be invaluable in confirming my clairvoyant diagnoses.

One example of this came was when I was healing a lady in her fifties, and I realised that she was absorbing the healing energy like a sponge. I asked if I could look at her hands, and was intrigued to find that the life line – which begins between the thumb and forefinger and would normally sweep outward towards the palm and down toward the wrist – had curved inward and was hugging the base of the thumb. This was a clear indication that her vital energy system was restricted.

It was during the course of one of our conversations that I realised she had an inborn negativity that would be very difficult to reverse, and that her health problems were a direct result of this factor, creating blockages that were preventing the intake and flow of the energy which sustains the physical body.

I asked if she would like to take part in an experiment to reform the negative thoughts by reversing them, so that she could see the problem as a whole and not from a totally negative viewpoint. I explained that no matter how bad she might perceive the problem to be, she could change that perception into something positive by looking at both cause and effect. There is no doubt at all that no matter how dire the situation, you can always find a glimmer of hope. The idea behind this experiment was to see whether the subconscious mind would eventually bring her problems to the surface of her waking mind. Fortunately, she agreed to co-operate.

She visited me once a month to clear the blockages in the energy system, and although she felt better in herself – and I could also see that change – the lines hadn't changed. However, as we moved into the fourth month, I could see faint minor lines emanating from the base of the life line towards the palm. This was a clear indication that the experiment was working. A year later, she no longer required healing because she had healed herself. She had completely reversed her negative condition and had developed a new set of lines with the power of her mind.

I have described this particular case so that you will understand how the subconscious mind interacts with the hand formations.

Many people's lives have been altered in this way. That is why it is important to remember that a negative reading does not have to mean a negative outcome. It is only the beginning.

If after reading this chapter you decide that you'd like to study palmistry, I would urge you to seek out a registered teacher. It is a subject that should always be treated with the utmost respect.

Another subject that you can study is graphology, or handwriting analysis, because handwriting is also affected by the mind and is another example of the significance of the mind/hand connection.

I have learned
To look on nature, not as in the hour
Of thoughtless youth; but hearing often-times
The still, sad music of humanity,
Nor harsh nor grating, though of ample power
To chasten and subdue. And I have felt
A presence that disturbs me with the joy
Of elevated thoughts; a sense sublime
Of something far more deeply interfused,
Whose dwelling is the light of setting suns,
And the round ocean and the living air,
And the blue sky, and in the mind of man.

Lines Composed a Few Miles Above Tintern Abbey
William Wordsworth 1770–1850

If you wish to receive distant healing, counselling, or a book and tape brochure, please write to the address below, enclosing a stamped and addressed envelope for the reply. Please keep letters as short as possible. Thank you.

Betty Shine
P.O. Box 1009
Hassocks
West Sussex
BN6 8XS

By the same author

MY LIFE AS A MEDIUM

Betty Shine has been a world famous medium for over 20 years and is highly respected for her remarkable powers and healing skills. Her extraordinary gifts have touched many hearts and inspired the lives of thousands of people from all walks of life. Yet, in spite of being guided by spirit voices from the age of two, Betty Shine admits she was initially reluctant to accept her personal destiny.

This is Betty's compelling story, describing an incredible personal journey from a career as an opera singer into the world of alternative healing and her poignant struggle to come to terms with her powerful gifts. In it, she shares some of the truly amazing and inspirational encounters she has experienced along the way, including astral travel, near death experiences, clairvoyant medical diagnosis and her discovery and study of Mind Energy.

'Betty's wisdom, down-to-earth attitude and sense of humour come across clearly through the pages of this book.'

Psychic News

ISBN 0-00-653138-5

By the same author

A MIND OF YOUR OWN

A Book for Life

A Mind of Your Own is a sourcebook for the millennium. Although the world changes around us, human beings never change — we experience the same thoughts, emotions and problems generation after generation.

In this book, Betty Shine uses over 200 carefully selected keywords to identify the most common anxieties which face people today — and then, drawing on her 20 years' experience of working as a medium and healer, she demonstrates how to overcome them. Now *you* can harness the potential of your own mind to improve your life and the lives of those around you.

Widely acclaimed as the most significant work of Betty Shine's long and distinguished career, *A Mind of Your Own* is a book both to read and to dip into. Nobody — from the ardent believer to the most hardened sceptic — can fail to be touched by the magic and the wisdom shared in this highly personal and deeply powerful book. It holds the power to change your life.

'Those who encounter Betty Shine's supernatural powers find it hard to remain sceptical'   *Independent*

ISBN 0-00-653019-2

By the same author

THE INFINITE MIND

The Mind/Brain Phenomenon

In the 25 years that Betty Shine has studied Mind Energy, the force that she herself discovered, the world of science has grown up. But scientists always make the same mistake; they fail to distinguish between the physical grey matter, the Brain, and the wonderful source of life itself, the Mind.

The Infinite Mind presents the proof for the existence of the Mind independent of the biological functions of the Brain. Drawing on a wide range of remarkable personal stories about survival evidence and contact with coma patients, including those involving celebrities from the worlds of entertainment and football, Betty Shine's irrefutable evidence and observations will inspire individuals from all walks of life to re-examine their beliefs.

'Betty is funny and warm, and there is nothing superhuman about her manner. But some of the things she takes for granted would send shivers down the normal spine.' *Daily Mail*

ISBN 0-00-653104-0